RUBBISH

Chris Barfoot
& Simon Klapish

The Authors

Simon Klapish

Simon Klapish grew up in Manchester, England, and then moved south to study Applied Biology at Plymouth Polytechnic. He migrated to Australia in 1982, served eleven years with the Australian Army Reserve, and gained a Masters Degree in Business (Marketing) at RMIT University. Simon lives in Melbourne with his wife, Leslie, and daughter, Emma. *Rubbish* is his third novel.

Also by Simon Klapish: *Ripples of Revenge* and *Chasing Margaret*

Chris Barfoot

A complex amalgamation of academic, scientist, engineer, artist, entrepreneur and father, Chris can be found wandering throughout Gippsland. He has published widely in obscure journals such as Industrial Robot. He is thought to be interested in motorcycles, photography, Kafkazian barbeques, archery and painting or since no one is quite sure about Barfoot, maybe not. He is noted for being pedantic, strange, eccentric, obscure, haughty and for being utterly inept and unreliable when it comes to writing autobiographical notes for his books.

Published in Australia by
Temple House Pty Ltd,
T/A Sid Harta Publishers
ACN 092 197 192
Hartwell, Victoria

Telephone:61 3 9560 9920
Facsimile:61 3 9545 1742
E-mail: author@sidharta.com.au

First published in Australia 2003
Copyright © Chris Barfoot and
Simon Klapish, 2003
Cover design, typesetting:
Chameleon Print Design
Cover illustration: Beau White

The right of Chris Barfoot and Simon Klapish
to be identified as the Author of the Work has
been asserted in accordance with the Copyright,
Designs and Patents Act 1988.

All rights reserved. No part of this publication
may be reproduced, stored in a retrieval system, or
transmitted, in any form or by any means without
the prior written permission of the publisher, nor be
otherwise circulated in any form of binding or cover
other than that in which it is published and without
a similar condition being imposed on the subsequent
purchaser.

National Library of Australia Cataloguing-in-
Publication entry:
Barfoot, Chris and Klapish, Simon
Rubbish
ISBN: 1-877059-52-8
264pp

Typeset in Adobe Caslon

It is said that laughter is the best medicine, and we certainly hope that this book proves that to be the case.

The primary aim of this first print run of '*Rubbish*' is to raise funds for worthy projects by a number of community organisations and service clubs.

The project is spearheaded by the Latrobe Group of Rotary Clubs in Rotary District 9820 who hope to raise funds for a Rotary Centennial project - an accommodation house for sick children and their families attending Latrobe Regional Hospital - and the Regional Cancer Care Centre at Latrobe Regional Hospital.

Other service organisations involved in the sale of this book will direct their proceeds to these causes and others.

If successful, subsequent print runs will allow us to direct proceeds to a wider net of worthy recipients.

We hope that you laugh loud and long and we thank you for your support.

Barry Dunstan
Project Coordinator
Rotary Club of Moe

Ken Peake
Assistant Governor
Rotary Latrobe Group, District 9820

Felix Pintado
Chief Executive
Latrobe Regional Hospital

Our Thanks

THIS BOOK EVOLVED FROM A STRANGE COLLABORATION process that spanned more than a year and eventually saw the light of day almost by accident. It started as a joke and evolved into a novel. Along the way we tested the quality of the work with a number of readers and critics, and received enough positive feedback that allowed us to believe that the 'beast' had legs. We'd therefore like to thank the following for reading the earlier drafts and making suitable comments and cheering us along; Jennifer B., Andrew Bett, Maria Creighton, Barry Dunstan, Clive Hurren, Meegan Kepert, Leslie K., Alison Madden, Peter Massey, Neil Lawson, Carl Stephenson and anyone else we've forgotten.

Dedication(s)

With two authors we need two dedications, we think...

SIMON'S DEDICATION: To Ken Corish, the funniest bloke I ever had the pleasure to share a house with as a student. A naturally talented comedian and musician who kept me in fits of laughter over lots of beer – a brother in arms, especially when we were legless.

CHRIS'S DEDICATION: Just occasionally you meet a person who inspires you in ways you never thought possible and in my case that was Mr. David Murphy Esq. Mate, you are a battler, a legend and a true Aussie fighting spirit. As Spock would have put it "Live long and prosper".

Secondly to my family, if you have read this you are probably looking at me in new light and I would just like to point out that all the shocking, vulgar, sexy, rude and gory bits were written by Simon. How Leslie puts up with him I'll never know.

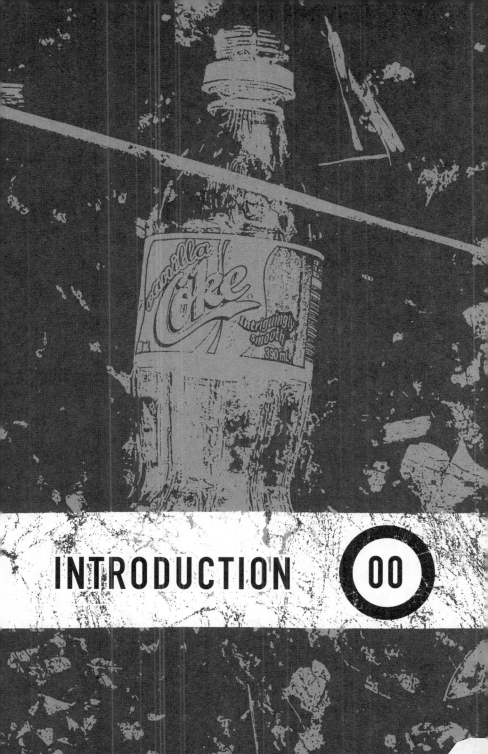

INTRODUCTION

00

Rubbish!

THERE LIES ANOTHER WORLD, UNKNOWN TO MANY of us, to which we contribute every day. A strange world that operates in the twilight of dawn and dusk, interacting with the general populace but once or twice a week. It is a world that many of us shun, trying desperately to avoid contact with it as much as possible. A world of strange smells, birds, rotting flesh and flies. A place where heavy machinery works continuously in an attempt to hide this obscenity whilst we try to ignore its existence.

Welcome to the world of the rubbish dump.

chapter

THERE IS AN OLD ITALIAN SAYING 'WHERE THERE'S muck, there's money' and this certainly applies to the rubbish business. People want to be rid of their rubbish and are willing to pay good money to have it removed. As consumerism continues to grow so does the production of rubbish, and so for a dump operator these are good times. Recycling is the flavour of the month, if not the decade, which provides another means to make money from the things that people throw away. Batteries, steel, plastic, paper and glass are all a terrific source of revenue rather than just land fill. Even dump sales have become popular, with people often shopping

for scrap or an antique and it's amazing what people will buy after a quick spit and polish. Unfortunately, despite these good times, not everything was bright in the business.

Dave's dump was located in a disused quarry, which much to Dave's disgust was filling up far too fast. It was obvious to him that soon there would be no room left to dump more rubbish and the cost of setting up a new site would be horrendous.

Yep, ever since the do-gooders in the form of the EPA had got involved it had become almost impossible to start up a good new dump. Nowadays you needed to have environmental impact studies, impervious linings, and all sorts of other controls. In the old days all you did was find a good hole, fill it up and move on to the next one. This business had been a good wicket for many years but now it seemed to be coming to the end of its innings.

Come to think of it, Dave's working life should also have been coming to an end. He was on the wrong side of fifty and his body showed the scars of a hard fought life. His left hand was more akin to a claw than a hand, after a set of tractor belts and pulleys had managed to amputate a couple of fingers. A receding hairline had now extended so far that he was often described as having a forehead that reached down to his arsehole. Pretty or handsome were never words used to describe Dave unless the sentence included the word 'not'. Now even his arms had proven to be too short and so he had to finally get himself reading glasses. It was amazing how many prescriptions there are and so it had taken nearly six months of collecting but he had finally found a pair that seemed to be right.

It's hard to describe the way that the townsfolk felt about Dave. Basically none liked him, but he provided a much-needed service, and so was tolerated in much the same way as the local prostitute, although small doses were preferable because wherever Dave travelled he brought along the distinctive odour of the rubbish tip. Even the local tennis club had banned him because despite taking a pre-match shower, as soon as he started to sweat, which was virtually with any movement, the odour along with the sweat oozed distastefully from his pores.

In a singles games this had been an advantage, particularly if the wind was blowing towards the opposition, but finding a doubles partner who could concentrate whilst on the court had been impossible. Mind you, Dave had always been a loner and so he never really cared about the opinion of others. As long as they came and paid the money to drop off their rubbish he was happy. And money was the only thing that really mattered to Dave. Well, almost the only thing. He did have a softer side, but he kept it well hidden. The name of his softer side, or rather his desire to win the elusive prize that would help develop his softer side, was Caroline. But for now Caroline was not on his mind.

'It can't end here. There has to be another way to extend the dump,' muttered Dave as he sat down in the old armchair he had recently rescued. This movement sent a cloud of flies into the air as his back contacted the chair, they circled briefly and then hovered nearby waiting for him to settle. It was a comfortable chair; only two springs were broken and the rats had yet to taste the delights of the tapestry covering, but even a luxury item like this did not help his state of mind. His business was in trouble and he knew that something had to be done and done fast. But what?

As he was contemplating his problem, his plant operator, Slim, blundered into the office, again making the flies buzz angrily around before settling on safe territory.

Slim was a local ex-Australian-rules football champion. In his prime he had been a real dog in the forward pocket. He'd never missed an opportunity to kick a ball, or a head. But now his career was languishing, along with his local club that was struggling to survive the amalgamation of the leagues. He was also starting to suffer from the results of the knee reconstructions and broken ribs incurred whilst playing, as well as the numerous hand and mouth injuries from the parties after the game.

Still, he was a striking figure. Continuous playing had kept him thin and Dave made sure that he kept his physical activity to a maximum whilst he was at the dump. Slim didn't really want to work at the dump but Mum had insisted that family had to help family. Technically Slim and Dave were half brothers although it was five husbands removed. But Mum had to be obeyed, something Dave and Slim knew all too well.

'I know what to do, Dave! I've worked out a solution,' he said with a beaming smile.

'What is it this time?' he sighed, waiting for yet another hair-brained scheme doomed to failure.

'Well, the only stumbling block to using our hole in the ground for that shipment of contaminated waste is the EPA finding out about it. So we just dump the crap at night, using a friendly driver, then bulldoze some clay on top of it to disguise it and then during the day shift we'll cover it more fully and no-one will know that it's there.'

'Don't you think it will become pretty obvious that the hole is filling up much faster than expected? The day shift aren't completely stupid you know,' replied Dave.

'But that's the beauty of it, because they are.' Slim said with a satisfied grin. 'They're as dumb as dog shit and spaced out on No Doze and caffeine from their night jobs on the side. They wouldn't know if the hole was full or empty half the time, they're too interested in the sick leave roster raffle.'

'Hmm,' pondered Dave, 'you may have a point there. After all their IQ is only marginally above idiot level, and their job commitment is similar to Mississippi slaves in the civil war. It could be worth a try. What do you suggest we bribe the night driver with to keep quiet?'

'I thought I'd promise him sex with my Tasmanian half-sister, she's always given me a good root!' exclaimed Slim.

Dave shook his head. 'But hasn't every driver had her already around here?' asked Dave.

'Yeah,' acknowledged Slim, 'but not since she's been cured and re-bored. She's like a virgin with experience now!'

'Okay let's try it. Get her on the phone and see if she's willing to enter into a monogamous arrangement for a change.'

Slim raced into the office to use the phone and Dave settled back into his chair thinking that all those stories about Tasmanians may be true after all, as he lovingly scratched his balls and contemplated the possibilities.

He muttered to himself, 'I mean the EPA call this stuff 'prescribed' waste and everyone knows that it takes a doctor to prescribe stuff and when they do it makes you feel better. Come to think of it the profit from this will make me feel better too. But it still won't be enough to keep the business running for more than another year.' His thinking was interrupted by a more urgent need, he lifted one cheek from the chair and let rip with a fart that reverberated throughout the dump.

'Perhaps methane?' he considered, taking in a deep breath and feeling the tang of that very gas all the way down his throat. This immediately brought on a spasm of coughing. The type of cough that any smoker will know can only be cured by another cigarette. He reached into the back pocket of his dungarees disturbing the flies again. Hoping that there was not too much methane lingering he flicked the lighter. No explosion? Good. He lifted the lighter to the cigarette. A deep drag brought on more coughing and he relaxed to contemplate the ideas running through his head.

'Methane could be good,' he said, talking to no-one in particular. His faithful blue heeler twitched her ears and rolled her eyes in his direction. 'But hmmm, to do that I'd need a lid.' Dave had seen one of these new-fangled devices when overseas on a 'study tour.' Oh what a tour that had been, all round the world drinking, wenching and occasionally pausing to look at pig shit or other dumps and then the whole cost was written off on his tax. The one that he had seen had just been a dump that had a lid. The material then rotted inside and the gas was trapped. A pipe could then be put through the lid and the gas tapped off. This could then be used to run a gas turbine and make electricity. He was surprised at how much he remembered of it especially given the amount of alcohol that had been consumed on that trip. The thought brought a smile to his lips. Here was another way to make money, he thought and money was the main thing in life to Dave. With enough money he could escape, and possibly with his secret love, but he quickly put those thoughts away, scared to even think them until the time was right.

Inspired, Dave went out and climbed into the tractor and backed it up to the tool shed. He fitted up the auger to the power take off and headed out into a disused part of the dump. As he drove he contemplated the possibilities. Rotting rubbish turned into electricity could be the answer. Everyone knew that there was huge money in the electricity business, otherwise how else could those bastards afford those big power plants?

Arriving at a likely spot he backed the tractor into position and set about drilling a hole. The auger bit into the ground and turned through the clay capping.

Dave kept his eye and lighter out for signs of gas and watched the top of the auger like a hawk. It passed through the clay and continued its downward journey. The first thing to come to the surface was a fine, white, stringy material. Dave suddenly remembered the few thousand tonnes of asbestos that he had buried there previously. He quickly filled in the hole and decided to abandon this particular area.

He moved back into a more recent area of the dump and tried again. The auger again attacked the surface. He watched carefully as the auger brought more things to the surface, used nappies, decaying vegetables, plastics and a dead cat. Well he thought it was a dead cat, it was hard to tell once the auger had twisted its way to the surface. Given that they don't have fur covered snakes anywhere he assumed it was a cat, or maybe it might have been one of those sausage dogs. Very long one though if it was. Either way it looked like a sausage now. But there was no sign of any methane.

'Damn,' he muttered at no one in particular. 'This shit is only good for the bloody worms!' He paused, then yelled 'WORMS, that's IT!' Jumping into the tractor he slapped it into gear and headed towards the office. The lack of forward progress puzzled him until he noticed that the auger was still in the ground. Once he lifted this he proceeded at a much faster pace.

Reaching the office he jumped out of the tractor and burst through the door screaming, 'I've got to get worms!'

Slim looked up from an edition of Playboy that

he had found on the dump earlier and muttered, 'Shouldn't be too hard working around here, we've got every other disease known to man.'

'No, you dickhead!' screamed Dave, 'Earthworms. Imagine a dump full of writhing, wriggling, squirming worms, zillions of them,' he paused with a glint in his eye, 'All of them busy eating the rubbish and turning it into worm shit that we can sell back to the punters and...., I don't even have to pay the bastards.' He looked hard at Slim.

Slim recognised that look in Dave's eye and knew that he'd better do some fast talking if was to avoid being replaced by an earthworm. Dave meanwhile was mentally comparing Slim to an earthworm, noting the similarity in build and their penchant to turn everything they get hold of into shit.

'Now come on, Dave,' said Slim, 'where would you get zillions of earthworms?' He paused, desperately trying to find a plausible reason. 'What about that stuff that comes in on the night shift, eh, not even a bloody worm could live in that let alone eat it.' Slim, now sweating profusely added, 'and what if the sun comes out, then they'd all be fried. Haven't you ever seen a cooked worm on the concrete?'

A flicker of doubt crossed Dave's face. The thought of a dump full of stiff, fried worms did not appeal, particularly if he had bought them. Besides if they did die they would become more stuff in his dump, which would fill it up even quicker. But the idea was so appealing.

'I know,' said Dave, 'when I was a kid we used to cut

a worm in half and it would grow into two worms. So all I need is a razor blade and one worm.'

Slim sensed a chance and dove in quickly. 'But that would take years, Dave, I mean you can only cut a worm into so many pieces and have it survive.'

'Hmmph,' muttered Dave and he retreated to his armchair to consider.

Slim had a point. If one worm cut in half took a week to grow into two worms, then in two weeks he'd have four worms, in three weeks, eight. Trouble is he needed millions of the little wriggling bastards and he didn't want to wait that long.

But what if he got them? How would he keep them here? I mean chasing worms was going to be like chasing a herd of cats only harder because worms went underground. Dave already knew how hard cats were. The fake fur business he started had been a great idea particularly as all those cats already came to him. But trying to round them up into the container attached to the exhaust of the old Valiant ute had never proven successful. The best he had managed so far was one large ginger tom, which to be honest seemed to have had serious suicidal tendencies and after a bit of taxidermy magic it now was a hat that Davy Crockett would be proud of. The tail reached down to the middle of his back and the head featured prominently at the front. Dave kept this cat hat aside for only the most special occasions.

No, making his own worms was not going to be successful. Damn. The idea was so good.

But what if you could build a mechanical worm? One machine that did what millions of worms did?

He sat back in the chair and pondered until dusk, his brooding only interrupted by the thump of passing garbage trucks hitting wombats.

Yeah, a big munching mechanical worm that could chew up all the rubbish and spit out stuff that you could sell to the punters. But how? A successful quick search under a number of pieces of long-term garbage and a quick vivisection with a butter knife demonstrated that there's not much in a worm that can be easily changed into mechanical bits.

This was going to need some thought, maybe another study tour even. Government sponsored perhaps?

Yes, he thought, it was time to buy a magnum bottle of scotch and go visit the local Member of Parliament again.

* * *

The local Member of Parliament opened the door to see Dave standing there. The smell hit him like a blanket, or possibly a more accurate description would have been like the way a dead and festering rat dripping ooze from open sores feels and smells as it physically hits one's face after being thrown at one by a very strong man.

John Brent MP recoiled and immediately rammed his hands into his pockets and brought white knuckles out, gripping a handkerchief in one hand and sneezing with gusto. The handkerchief remained in place.

'Dave, good to see you,' the MP coughed. 'Why don't we talk in the garden, as it's such a nice night,' he said hurriedly, looking briefly at the sky and ignoring the odd drops of rain that belied his description. He closed the front door behind him. 'What's up, Dave?' he said as he furtively looked up and down the street.

'I need to go on a tour of foreign tips, to get some competitive intelligence on worm farming. It's a great investment opportunity that will benefit the state economy and bring countless benefits to the, er, industrial sectors that need better management of waste processes, and, er…' Dave paused, trying to get more of the right sounding words and phrases that he knew government types needed so that they could agree to a taxpayer funded jaunt.

'Okay, okay, Dave. Don't labour the bloody point. Cut to the chase,' the MP said through his handkerchief. 'Where do you want to go and for how long?'

'Good,' Dave said, visibly relaxing, knowing immediately that his previous campaign funding was going to provide further dividends. 'Paris, for a fortnight,' he announced with a smile.

'Paris?' the MP asked with some disbelief. 'Why Paris?'

'Well,' Dave began, 'I've read that they have a pretty good city dump and apparently they have one of the world's biggest worm farming ventures there. Anyway, why do you care?' he added with some indignation.

'It's expensive, that's why. I have to justify these things you know. Questions will be asked,' the MP said with an air of superiority that immediately annoyed Dave.

'Really? What kind of questions?' Dave asked but then continued, 'you mean questions like what was the name of the seventeen year old schoolgirl that likes to cuddle up with a local Parliamentarian behind the bike sheds on Wednesday sports afternoons when there's no-one looking? Or maybe questions like who was the bookie that was asked to forget about some badly advised horse race investments made by a local dignitary? Or perhaps...'

'Okay,' the MP hissed, 'you've made your point. When do you want to go?' he sighed in resignation.

'Next week will do nicely,' Dave said with a smile. 'Oh, and John, business class, mate,' he winked.

As Dave departed down the garden path he could faintly hear the sound of someone retching into the flowerbeds.

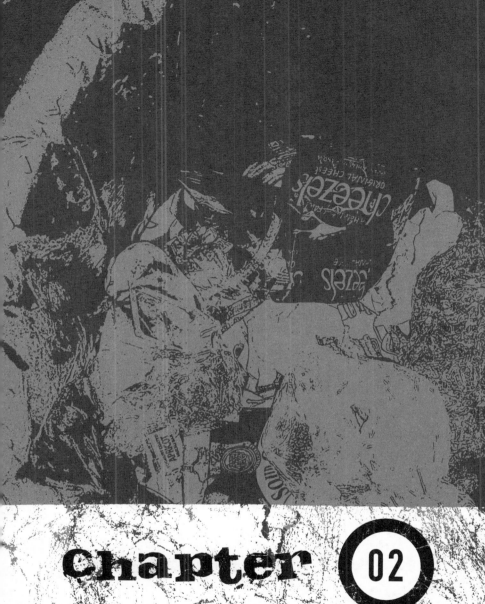

chapter 02

DAVE HAD NEVER BEEN VERY GOOD AROUND PEOPLE, or was it that people just didn't like being around Dave? Either way, for the 450 people trapped on the same overseas flight, it was an experience that they would never forget. From that time on, whenever they smelled a particularly noxious odour, drain cleaner, septic tanks, oven cleaner, or ammonia for instance, they would remember that seemingly never-ending flight. Yes, sea travel, no matter the cost, or the time, or the ship, even the Titanic, was likely to be preferable in the future for those people.

Airport security will also long remember his visit. 'Sarin gas' the detector had said. Emergency evacuation, news crews, the SAS abseiling in from helicopters, tracker dogs picking up his trail but choosing to stay ten metres upwind to bark at him and those poor drug sniffer dogs that they think will never work again. Dave still thought that they should have had the courtesy to remove the gas masks when they interviewed him. They were at least polite and refrained from doing the full body search, muttering something about not being able to get a volunteer, even from the SAS. Once convinced that the reaction from the detectors came purely from a complete overload of its sensors they were most apologetic and let him continue. Indeed they even insisted on providing him an escort to the plane.

For Dave, once aboard the plane, he was at last able to relax. It was nice to be away from the dump. There's nothing like visiting strange exotic countries and checking out what they throw away, particularly when someone else was paying, he thought.

Yep, his Member of Parliament had been great, he had even openly stated that sending him overseas would do Australia a great public service. Marvellous man that MP, and it felt so nice to be appreciated.

The plane smelt just like the dump. All the other passengers sitting nearby would pause at regular intervals, grab a bag and heave up whatever they had left in their stomachs. Much like most of the visitors that came to drop stuff off at the dump. Dave couldn't help but wonder what company got the job of cleaning up all those bags. Good stuff vomit, completely degrades, taking up no space in the dump.

He was still nervous about leaving Slim in charge. There always had been the suspicion that most of the good rubbish ended up in Slim's shed at home. It had never been proven though. Mind you, Slim had built three extensions on that shed in the last year. A close inspection would be required once he got back.

Dave's aim on this tour was to party as hard as he could and in between visit a number of sites and see how they convert their garbage into products. His personal aim was to maximise the first activity and minimise the second. Basically though he was looking for a company that made the equivalent of a mechanical worm and if he had to search the ends of the earth to find it, great!

After a lifetime of flying, or that's how it felt to those nearby, they touched down in France where Dave had based the first part of the study tour.

Now France has always been a country known for its hospitality, or is it hostility? But somehow they just seemed to match Dave's temperament exactly. He really just felt at home there. The politeness of the waiters equalled his own and the courtesy of the hotel staff reminded him of how he treated the punters at home. Yes, after a week in a Parisian hotel he was sure that 'Fawlty Towers' was in fact a documentary series and Basil was based on a Parisian manager.

The warm balmy days were spent wandering the city taking in the sights. Occasionally he would pause and rummage through a nearby bin looking for any opportunity that may present itself.

The evenings were a time to stroll and take in the 'atmosphere' at places such as the Moulin Rouge and the various red light districts.

Late one night Dave was wandering along the banks of the Seine when he saw a bevy of beauties standing under the bridge near Notre Dame Cathedral, smoking pungent cigarettes and wearing very short skirts and high-heeled boots. Must be tourists he thought. Then one of them approached him, but as she got closer she started to gag and cough and hurriedly retreated back to her sisters in the shadows. Some rapid French ensued and then one of them, who seemed to have a shocking head cold came over and said 'Deux cent francs, monsieur. Voudrez vous enculer avec moi?'

'What's that doll-face?' Dave replied, not knowing a word of French.

Luckily the tart knew enough languages to make a decent living from most tourists, 'You are Eenglish?'

'Christ no! I'm no bloody Pom, I'm an Australian.'

'Oh, that is good. Do you want to screw me, for 200 francs?'

'What? Oh, I see. Seems a lot of money to me, but it's been a long time, with someone else anyway, why not. Where will we do it?'

'Just here if you like, it's a warm night and the river is romantic, no?' Besides, she didn't want to go anywhere with this dirt bag, her colleagues had explained that she was the only one able to service this scum, because of the head cold and the fact she couldn't smell him. The others had disappeared as soon as the transaction was in progress, knowing that Monique rarely missed a sales opportunity and had earned the nickname of the golden pussy, or 'chat d'or' in the area.

As it turned out she almost regretted the time spent, even for such a sum of money. He was gross and inept, but very quick at least, and she managed to steal another few hundred francs from him whilst he slept and snored under the bridge afterwards.

Dave awoke poorer but more relaxed. Come to think of it sleeping on the footpath under the bridge was much like his bed at home.

But all good things come to an end and Dave eventually found it impossible to further delay looking at the various planned garbage sites. The first visit was to a worm farm. He knew he was actually going to have to visit the farm and write up a report, otherwise the government wouldn't cough up with the money for another tour next time and he wanted to make sure that there would be a next time. The weather was going to be crap, which seemed appropriate, as Dave didn't wish to waste a good day working. So he hired a small car and set out, complaining all the time about the steering wheel and the traffic being on the wrong side. How he made it through the traffic of Paris is still unknown and best attributed to the phrase 'the devil looks after his own.'

Once in the countryside he could proceed at a gentler pace. Winding his way through the hills, with the occasional swerve to get on to the right side, he watched the storm gather until he came upon his destination. As he heaved his weight out of the little car a man in a white coat came over.

'Bonjour, my name is Jacques,' he greeted the arrival. 'Are you Dave from Australia?'

'Yeah, that's me, G'day,' replied Dave, thinking to himself that this bloke looked like a pox doctor's clerk. He paused and scratched himself thinking that after last night's encounter he may need to visit one of those on a more professional basis.

'Ahh Dave, I am the manager here and your embassy has arranged for me to show you around,' said Jacques. 'I have been expecting you here for the last week or zo, did you have trouble in Paris?' he asked.

Dave squirmed 'Ahh, actually I was enjoying the French hospitality and the great atmosphere of the place'.

Jacques smiled a knowing smile 'Oui Dave, that is the romance of Paree. No-one cannot be moved by her beauty and charm. Still you came to see worms, not to listen to me, zo follow me to ze factory and see what we have done.'

'OK,' mumbled Dave. He was just grateful to get inside as the large storm clouds closed in overhead.

Inside was a huge worm farm, tray upon tray of the little blighters reaching to the roof of the ten metre high building. The pungent earthy aromas filled the building as the worms ate the crap that they put in and converted it to what they called 'vermicast,' which was just a fancy way of saying worm shit. Dave pondered on this. It seemed that if they have something that is disgusting and that no one could move, then they give it either a foreign or fancy name. I mean escargots sound pretty good, but you try and sell snails at the local pub.

'Hmm,' Dave muttered, wondering if the same applied to beverages, 'perhaps I'll get off the Chardonnay and stick to beer. Yep, if it's got four letters, it must be good.'

But the worms just didn't look good. The place was clean, with little smell compared to the dump back home; jeeze, it felt almost like a hospital.

'No bloody way could I live here,' Dave said. His mood wasn't helped by memories of the pre-school worm eating contest when, as a four year-old, Dave had gone head to head with the curly haired blonde, Lois. It had been neck and neck but at ninety-nine Dave had succumbed to the wriggling in his stomach and he had lost the lot. Lois meanwhile chomped down on number one hundred and took the title. Dave had never felt the same about worms since. Sometimes just the thought of them made him want to retch.

Meanwhile, Jacques continued down the pathway between the towering stacks of trays. 'Zo you see, Dave, we introduced ze bowel solids into ze trays via zese lines here and then we collect ze vermicast from ze base of ze tower here,' he said as he wandered along pointing out all aspects of the operation.

Dave paused. 'So you get paid to take the crap and then these… worms, turn it into worm shit and you get paid for that also.'

Jacques nodded, 'Zat is right Dave, we get paid on ze way in and on ze way out. Good, n'est pas?'

Dave nodded, 'Yeah, it seems OK. I mean you're getting money both ways but what does it cost you?'

'Zat is ze beauty of it all,' said Jacques. 'Zey cost zo little, no food, no wages, no holidays; it iz ideal.'

Dave was impressed. Not with the worms, he hated those bastards, but the money, yeah maybe this guy was onto something here. No overheads, low running costs, getting paid to take shit and to give it back. It seemed too good to be true.

He stopped. 'Jacques,' he called, 'this sounds too good. What can go wrong? Can you get some bad shit and they all die? Do they fry up on the concrete? Or what?'

Jacques turned to him, 'No Dave, zese are the same worms that have lived for hundreds of years in the earth. Zey are strong! Nothing can affect them.'

Just then there was an almighty clap of thunder. Jacques looked concerned. 'Oh, perhaps I did speak too zoon,' he said. 'Zere is one thing that they do not like.' They moved to the door, watching as sheets of lightning appeared across the sky and the thunder roared deafeningly.

Jacques turned back inside and screamed 'Non! Merde! Mon ami, help me,' and ran desperately to the trays of worms.

Dave sauntered along behind, not seeing any reason to rush. But as he got closer to Jacques he could see the problem. The worms were evacuating the area. Wow! The worms wanted to get out of there. Tray after tray of worms all bent on escape desperately trying to bail out and get away.

'What the bloody hell is going on?' screamed Dave. Lucky to be heard as more deafening claps of thunder crashed in from overhead.

'Zee worms, Dave, zey do not like the lightning!' yelled Jacques as he desperately grabbed handfuls and stuffed them into any available pockets. 'When zis happens, zey run away. I must stop them! Quick, Dave help me!' said Jacques, who by now was starting to look like a extra from 'Night of the Living Dead' as worms seemed to be oozing from every orifice and body part and more just kept pouring out of the trays.

'Zis is my worst nightmare, when ze worms they do not want to be here anymore, and zey run away,' said Jacques. Dave agreed, Jacques was starting to look more and more like his worst nightmare as well.

'Uh, looks like the weather's improving,' said Dave as more thunder crashed, lightning ripped across the sky and the rain hammered down even harder. 'Gotta go mate, gotta see a man about a dog!' he yelled as he rushed for the car.

Once inside the car, wet and frozen, he sat and shuddered, partly from the cold and partly from images of a worm infested Jacques that kept running through his mind. Worms were no longer considered a real option for Dave's dump.

The drive back was equally interesting. With the weather so atrocious and Dave not used to left hand drive, nothing but pity can be felt for those that occupied the same piece of road as Dave that day.

The next day Dave sat at breakfast and pondered how he could have gone through so much of the study tour money in just a few days in this city. Even a Cabinet Minister would have trouble achieving an expenditure rate like this, he considered. But he was excited to be going to the Paris main dump later that morning with a local official even if he was going to have to cut the rest of his planned trip short, which mainly consisted of relaxing on the Mediterranean coast, due to a lack of funds.

When Dave met his guide at the dump they became instant friends, achieved from an immediate and deep mutual professional affinity. Here at last was another man who could appreciate the intricacies of garbage. Someone else who was also able to immediately assess at a glance the contents of a green garbage bag. His name was Henri and he was an interesting character. It was obvious from his deep sun tan that he had spent a lot of time outdoors and his well-muscled frame suggested that he had done a lot of physical work. It was hard to estimate his age, but Dave guessed that he would be in his mid forties and he still cut a fine figure. Whilst the two men were deep in mutual respect for each other and their peculiar profession, after having spent some time getting their hands dirty in the up-market garbage of Paris, Henri made a suggestion to Dave that was to change his life.

'Monsieur Dave, I av a bizness proposal for you that will mek you very rich, if you can do eet'

'Spell it out mate, money's my middle name,' said Dave, suddenly taking an even deeper interest in Henri.

'How would you like to take some of our waste

from one of our Pacific Islands, a friendly little place called Mururoa?'

The name sounded familiar but Dave was never good at geography and had a vague feeling that there was a Club Med resort there or something. 'Don't give a shit where stuff comes from really, just what it's worth to me. How much is there and how much will you pay, and will it take up much room?'

'No, no, not much room at all, and we'll deliver it in steel boxes, heavy ones, and we'll pay you $500 for each box, but you must smuggle them from the ship to your dump,' Henri explained.

'Why do you need to smuggle them in?' asked Dave.

Henri shook his head. 'It is ze Government, Dave. Zere tip charges are too 'igh.'

Dave nodded. He knew how much the various government agencies ripped out of him for their licences, but it still sounded a little fishy.

'How big is a box?' asked Dave, still worried about the rapid filling of the dump.

'Very small, Dave, about ze size of a chocolate box, zey will take up very little room,' said Henri, reading Dave's concern.

'Make it a thousand bucks a box and I'm in,' Dave haggled. 'At that price you can let me worry about the smuggling part, I can handle that too.'

Henri made a pretext of thinking about it, but even $1,000 was incredibly cheap. 'Okay then, you have a deal,' he said with a smile.

'How many boxes are there then?' Dave asked.

'Oh, we can send you maybe a hundred over the next few months if you like?'

Shit, a hundred, at $1,000 each that's a hundred thousand bucks, GST free, tax free, bloody hell, I've hit the jackpot, Dave thought. Then some doubts crept into his head, 'Why pay so much for some boxes? What's in them and why don't you bring them here?'

'Oh, it's too far to bring them here and the airfares are very expensive and no ships want to deal with little boxes these days, they are only interested in containers.'

It sounded plausible, and Dave didn't even notice that Henri's accent had sort of disappeared as the deal was progressing, but all he could think of was the money now. 'Okay, you've got a deal, mate.'

Henri looked very happy and the two of them spent the rest of the day touring the various areas of the dump. Henri taught him to distinguish between the rubbish bags of the rich and famous and those from the poorer districts. Dave reciprocated by demonstrating his technique of always ensuring that the richer bags were emptied last thus spreading their contents over a larger area and making it easier to go shopping. It was a blissful time and they played and talked throughout the day each revelling in the joy of finding a real soul mate.

Dave reluctantly booked his return flight

that very afternoon. Stuff the worms he thought, I'm in the little steel box game now. Daft French, don't know what things cost at all. Henri was to ship a preliminary set of 10 boxes later that month to make sure all was okay and then he'd start to send bigger shipments he said.

Dave was much, much happier than the passengers sitting near him on the Air France flight to Singapore that night. He had a few problems with the airport people in Singapore when he was connecting to the Qantas flight home though.

As soon as they scanned his passport number something came up on the screen and then the bastards escorted him away. They made him take a shower and gave him new clothes and confiscated his old ones, said there was a con-tamination scare or something. 'Little pricks,' thought Dave, 'and to think people complained about the French.'

So it was an unfamiliar Dave that boarded the jumbo for the journey home. His adjacent passengers will never know what they missed. Indeed if anyone ever writes a book on airline near-catastrophes this may be recorded as one and it certainly stands as an excellent example of the benefits of Internet communication.

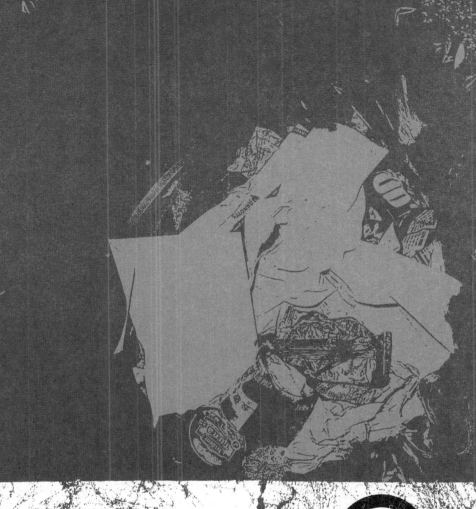

chapter 03

The day after his return to Australia, Dave arrived at the dump early. Well, early morning Paris time that is. In terms of eastern standard Australian time it was more like 2:00pm. The sun had already reached its peak, bringing alive those odours usually reserved for abdominal surgeons. Odours that simply have to be experienced rather than described, but it made Dave feel at home, and thankfully there wasn't a worm in sight.

Nothing seemed to have changed much since

he left. As he drove the ute in to the dump he watched another customer pause while empty-ing the trailer to vomit next to the wheel. The large yellow tractor with the steel wheels rolled calmly over a television that immediately im-ploded. A nearby part of the trench collapsed, taking an old Morris Minor complete with grandmother dressed in a bowls uniform with it. The old blue heeler raced out, snapped at the back wheel of his car and ducked behind it as it passed, blissfully unaware that he was towing a trailer.

Yes, life seemed pretty much the same as ever.

He drove over towards the shack and parked outside. Getting out he breathed deeply, drawing that pungent aroma into his lungs. 'Hmm, home at last,' he said and headed over to the shack.

He opened the door of the shack and yelled, 'Slim, you lazy bastard, wake up! Where are you?' Pausing for a moment he surveyed the dump, looking for any changes that may have occurred. His eyes focused on a point where it appeared that the ground level was lower, could it be that someone had been taking rubbish out of his dump? Never!

The flies by now had noticed his return and they quickly resumed their familiar position.

'Slim!' he roared, and this time he received a reaction from somewhere deep inside the shack.

A clatter of chairs rang out and Slim emerged, blinking sleepily into the light.

'Oh, g'day, Dave. Didn't expect you back so soon,' muttered Slim trying his best to appear as if he'd been awake all the time.

'What's that!' Dave exclaimed pointing to the depression in the dump.

Slim paused and appeared to study the point intently. 'Dunno Dave, but give it a couple more days and we should be able to tell from the skeleton.'

'It's your bloody skeleton they'll find!' screamed Dave, 'I mean over there where some bastard has been removing MY rubbish.'

'Oh that,' muttered Slim suddenly developing an extreme interest in the toes of his boots.

'Well...' drawled Dave, not so much pausing for dramatic reasons but rather due to the fact that his mind was very preoccupied with potential retributions that could be applied to Slim.

Slim had by now broken out in a serious sweat. 'Well, you know that old guy that comes here, brings in a trailer load and takes home two.'

'Yeah,' said Dave fondly, as this guy was one of their best customers; polite and he always paid well for the extras he took home.

'Well,' continued Slim, 'he bought a vintage car and was in desperate need of some bits. As he was such a good customer we helped him out cos we had one buried right there,' he said, pointing to the depression.

Dave couldn't remember ever planting cars in that spot; it usually had been scrap steel. But he had been away for a while and anything might have come in. 'Okay,' he said, 'but now I've got to think what I could put in that hole...' He paused, suddenly inspired.

'Don't worry Slim, just get the excavator and open that hole up a bit more will you?' he asked, a large grin beginning to crease his face, 'Make it a couple metres across and about three down.'

Slim, never one to look a gift horse in the mouth, sprinted for the excavator at breakneck speed. As he collapsed into the drivers chair he said to himself, 'Jesus I hope he never comes to a home football match, cos if he ever sees the steel in that new grandstand I'm dead meat.' Slim did have a point. The new grandstand had been constructed using mainly scrap steel and chairs that Slim had collected over the years from the dump. This is the collection that had filled his shed for so long. The other thing that might give it away was the fact that it had been named the Slim Memorial Grandstand. He hadn't been happy with the name but the committee had pointed out that it simply saved them the trouble of having to rename it when and if he died. This did seem to make sense in some sort of strange and twisted way and so he had gone along with it.

He moved the excavator into position and started to dig deeper, into something that defies description, so…well, grossly yuk that it must be left to the imagination.

Dave meanwhile moved into the office. Nothing much here had changed. His armchair was still there and a few more recently reclaimed 'gentlemen's magazines' decorated the desktop. He picked up one and tried to flip through it but most of the good pages were stuck together. Still, not even this was going to upset him now. Slim had provided him with the perfect spot to put those steel boxes that were due soon. Sure, Henri had said to spread them around, but that was Paris, this was an Australian tip and what works here is different to there. 'Yep,' he decided, 'a single hole with all those boxes stacked one on top of the other would be ideal'.

'Now, how can we get those boxes here?' pondered Dave.

chapter 04

Now whilst Dave may be considered to be an enemy to all that is green, Achmed and Yousef were simply an enemy to all.

These two were the most feared terrorists of all time. Osama was but a playground bully compared to them. Life meant absolutely nothing to them. They had killed and tortured, maimed and kidnapped, hijacked and bombed. But now they were in search of the ultimate revenge on humanity. One final act was needed, one that would emblazon their names upon the pages of history forever. Something so disgusting that they could only be compared to Hitler, and even then with Hitler coming second.

'By the rabid dung of a thousand camels, Achmed, we must come up with an idea worthy of our place in history,' said Yousef.

Achmed paused to throw another knife into one of the many portraits of world leaders. 'You are right, Yousef. Fame and infamy cannot be ours without a deed so foul that we shall be remembered for all time. But what?'

Yousef pulled a pistol and added a third eye to the picture of the American President. 'We could assassinate a world leader,' he mused.

'NO!' cried Achmed, 'it has been done many times. By the prophet's beard what we need is something unique, something so foul that it has never been done, even by American school children.'

'We could bomb something?' pondered Yousef.

'Do not be as foolish as an Englishman in the desert. Everyone has bombed things; churches, planes, presidents, cities, all have been bombed,' he responded. He paused thoughtfully, 'but no individuals have ever used a nuclear bomb.'

Yousef leaped to his feet, 'By the spleens of a hundred mongoose. What genius, that is what we shall do. One large device destroying a major city and writing our name in the stars.'

'But where can we obtain the material we need to construct such a device?' asked Achmed.

Yousef leaned back holding his finger against his nose, 'Ah Achmed, I have a friend in Paris who has many contacts, if anyone can find us this material it is Henri. Let us make the arrangements and go and pay him a visit.'

chapter (05)

'DAVE, I LOOK LIKE A DICKHEAD,' WHINED SLIM, 'and I'm getting seasick.'

Dave threw back his yard long pigtail and felt no pity whatsoever. 'Ah, shut up ya mongrel and start hauling up those flags.'

The day had started well. They had launched the boat late in the evening and travelled out beyond the bay under the cover of darkness. Here they met the French ship at about three in the morning, exactly as per Henri's instructions. They had then transferred ten small boxes to his boat and then both boats had gone their separate ways. These boxes might be small, but the things were way heavier than he'd expected, Dave thought.

As morning was breaking it was time to implement Dave's plan to avoid customs or police inspections at the dock.

The plan was simple. Not bright, but simple.

Dave's idea was to pretend that he was an anti-nuclear protestor complaining about warships coming into the bay, make a nuisance of himself and then when they were sick of him he would sneak back to shore. However, neither Dave nor Slim really looked the feral type that would lead this type of protest. Some serious rummaging through the rubbish had been required. This had turned up a collection of items that they used as a disguise.

Now adorned with that collection of odds and ends Slim did look better. He had a wig that looked like a leftover from the black power era, an absolutely pure afro at least two feet high. Dave had a long blonde pigtail that reached to his waist. The clothes they were wearing had been rescued from garbage brought in by the local charity, second-hand clothes shop. Nature and years of working at the dump had already endowed them both with that five-fortnights-in-the-forest freshness associated with a feral. Slim was now busy applying the camouflage to the boat.

Well, camouflage is probably not the best description as the boat was far from hidden. Slim was putting up the rainbow banners and the 'No Nukes' flags all over the ship. Along one side was a banner saying 'Save our hospital' which wasn't really appropriate but no one had thrown out anything better.

But the thing that really upset Slim was the fake jewellery.

Now everyone knows that a real feral has more holes than a crumpet and thus if these two were going to be even slightly believable they had to look the part. Unfortunately Slim was less than cooperative when Dave produced a darning needle from the bin of the local sewing shop. Slim, in the interest of less pain offered to buy some clip on rings.

With five of these down each ear and one on each nipple they looked more the part. But the ones that hurt were the ones in his 'private parts.' Dave had insisted on these in case they were strip-searched. Thus Slim had a bolt around his slug and to say that it was uncomfortable was an understatement. The combination of bolt, ill fitting pants and vigorous movement left him wondering if he'd ever be able to perform again without a ninety-degree bend in the old fella.

Slim speculated for a while on the likely benefit of such a modification and tried to determine the best direction for such a bend but the topic was all too difficult and he gave up.

'Heads up!' yelled Dave; 'I can hear it coming.'

'What do you hear?' replied Slim peering into the gloom. Suddenly a dark shape emerged from the fog. It was a large Collins class submarine, one of a number of diesel-powered submarines that were the pride of the Australian fleet, having only cost the tax-payers more than twice their original budget.

Dave fired the engines and thrust the boat forward. 'Lets do it,' he called.

The boat leapt after the submarine, coming alongside as she entered the heads.

'Go home, Yankee!' cried Slim ignoring the Royal Australian Navy flag displayed from the conning tower.

'Piss off, dickhead!' came the reply from the conning tower.

'No nukes!' yelled Dave.

'It's a frigging diesel!' came the reply.

Despite this completely nonsensical situation Dave kept harassing the sub, cutting in and out near the coning tower and bounding over the wake. The crew was by now all in favour of live weapon testing but the commander decided that it would be more politically correct to call in the water police.

This turned out to be an unfortunate decision

as the media had their scanners set to the police frequencies but what was even worse was that it was a very slow news day. So far the headlines for that morning revolved around the sexual exploits of two dogs that had outshone the political dignitaries at the previous night's opening of a new freeway. But here was something that whilst not news could at least possibly be made to look like news.

Soon the submarine's crew was further harassed by the arrival of a number of news helicopters that started to circle it mercilessly.

Dave's solo exploit protesting about nuclear power by harassing a diesel powered sub soon became the lead story on all the morning breakfast shows.

* * *

Anthena Treehugger, the leader of Greentrees was enjoying a well-earned sleep after a difficult night protesting at a local political launch. But that came to an end with the incessant ringing of the phone.

'Anthena, quick turn on the television,' screamed her sister Ima.

'Why?' mumbled Anthena.

'Just do it!' screamed Ima.

'What channel?'

'ANY BLOODY CHANNEL!' yelled Ima.

Anthena leaned over and turned on the television. The first thing she saw was a small boat occupied by what looked like two of her associates protesting about a nuclear sub. Although she didn't understand the significance of the 'Save our Hospital' sign she assumed that it must be a personal statement.

But why were they annoying what was clearly an Australian diesel submarine? Unless they had discovered something that proved the government had been lying all the time. She couldn't take that chance and reached for the phone.

'Hello, Greentrees, how can I help you?' a sleepy male voice answered.

'Tristan, it's me, Anthena, launch the boats and get out there to support the protest in the bay,' said Athena in a no-nonsense voice.

'Yes, ma'am,' said Tristan, hanging up and then implementing a well-oiled plan.

It wasn't long before Dave and Slim found themselves in the middle of a circus comprising a sub being circled by helicopters, water police and a flotilla of small boats and surfers.

Anthena by now had joined the protest and assumed control from one of the Greentrees boats. Her first task was to seek out the people that had started the protest.

'Ahoy there!' cried Anthena to Dave and Slim 'What are you doing?'

'We're protesting about nuclear powered subs,' screamed Dave.

'But this is a diesel sub,' called Anthena.

'Are you sure?' replied Dave.

Anthena paused. Could he be right? 'Tristan pull alongside their boat and then get a Geiger counter!' she called.

'Just wait while we check,' called Anthena to Dave as her boat manoeuvred alongside.

Tristan disappeared below deck and passed her the counter. She turned it on and the needle jumped to the far right stop, nearly wrapping itself around the post whilst emitting a constant scream.

'Sweet Jesus, he's right,' whispered Anthena. Tristan saw the result, went deathly pale, crossed himself and headed below deck to try and find a radiation suit.

She looked across to Dave, 'OK we'll handle it from here, you've done your duty, and thanks.'

Dave, grateful to be offered any opportunity to get away from the circus, waved and headed for shore whilst the environmental warriors set about significantly escalating an already crazy situation. 'Slim, my boy, the time has come for us to go forth and multiply, as they put it in the bible,' said Dave. And that is precisely what they did.

It was a slow and uneventful trip to shore. They removed the banners, the wigs and finally the ear, nose and nipple rings, making the ship and them look 'normal' again.

Once in the dock they loaded the boat on the trailer and headed back to the dump. It was a slow drive but Dave was happily contented and didn't even complain as they made their way home. Once there, Dave backed the boat into the shed ready to unload the cargo. He got out and then made his way to the side of the shed and swung the overhead gantry into place. Slim hit the 'lower' button and slowly guided the electro-magnet over the boxes. As it was just above knee height Dave flicked the switch and activated the magnet.

'Turn it off, turn it off!' screamed Slim, suddenly remembering that he hadn't removed the bolt from around his slug and was now undergoing a rapid penile extension program.

Dave deliberately hesitated for as long as could be considered reasonable, then counted to three, slowly, and threw the switch. 'Jesus Slim, if you're going to be like that unload it yourself and bury them one on top of the other in that hole you dug. I'm going home.'

Dave wandered back to office and put away all the items that he'd used for the boat trip and then packed up and started to leave the office. As he did, the TV that lived in the corner blasted the report, in glorious black and white, about the arrest of the Greentrees protestors this morning.

They even had a passing interview with their leader who was screaming, 'It's all a Government lie, a nuclear conspiracy, I saw the readings myself,' as two burly policemen dragged her to the divisional van.

chapter 06

HENRI WAS EXCITED TO SEE ACHMED AND Yousef again. Excited in the same way that a rat is excited when it is dropped in a tank full of cobras. Henri knew that these two were evil incarnate and that nothing could stand in their way, especially him. Dealing with these two, no matter how successfully you bargained, was always going to be like playing Russian roulette with a semi-automatic pistol.

'Ah Henri, merchant of many things, we have

come to ask that you help us procure some material for our next, er, project,' said Yousef.

'And what is zis project?' asked Henri.

Achmed paused and leaning back in the chair said, 'We are building a small bomb.'

Henri jumped to his feet 'Oui, oui, I can help you,' he said, opening the drawers of his desk, 'what is it that you would like; C4, Semtex, Plastique?'

'Do not bother us with playthings,' said Achmed, as he leaned forward, 'we want plutonium,' he said, fixing Henri with a withering stare.

Henri visibly recoiled as that word impacted upon him. 'Plutonium?' He paused and slumped back into his seat in shock. 'A nuclear bomb? Are you mad? No one will ever get away with such an action; the authorities will hunt you down to the ends of the earth.'

'Maybe we do not wish to get away,' said Yousef.

Henri was by now seriously scared. These two were fanatical enough and mad enough to conduct a suicide bomb mission using a nuclear device. My God, what a thought, but where would they attack? Surely not Paris! This was the centre of civilised life! London, well that would be OK, it would avenge the defeat by Henry the fifth. Sure it had been six hundred years ago but to the French, Agincourt was a festering wound. Berlin? Well, that would make up for the last two world wars. Washington? Destroying that could be a civil service to the whole world. If the target was to blow up Moscow, no-one would even notice. Everyone would simply assume that they never did sort out that Y2K issue on their missiles. Either that or the Premier had simply sacked another Government in a more dramatic way. Merde, the only thing to do is to get them as far away as possible from his beloved France.

'Well, gentlemen,' Henri began, with a smile returning to his face as his plan formed, 'I do have a small supply of ten, fifty kilogram boxes.'

Achmed and Yousef looked at each other quickly calculating the damage that would do. The original bomb dropped on Nagasaki had been eight kilograms and that had been equivalent to twenty-five kilotonnes of TNT and had caused death up to 1.5 kilometres from the epicentre. Fifty kilograms would equal about 156 kilotonnes of TNT and that could easily destroy any city in the world with up to a hundred thousand deaths.

'That would be enough,' said Yousef, nodding as he continued to imagine the effect that such a device would have.

'Unfortunately,' continued Henri, 'it is far from here, in a place that no one will suspect.'

'What do you mean? Where is it?' asked Achmed, icily as reached to his shoe where a small knife was hidden.

Henri beamed, 'Obviously I do not keep such materials here. It is hidden in a special storage in Australia,' he replied. 'However you will have to deal with the occupier of the site.'

Yousef looked menacing, 'That will not be a problem, we will deal with the infidel and any-one else that stands in our way,' he said fixing his gaze on Henri.

Henri smiled, thinking that there was no longer a need to bother about writing that cheque for Dave, as it would simply go to his estate. 'Let us work out a price and then I will give you the details, contacts and location.'

Chapter 07

Rubbish!

It was a pleasant drive home and Dave felt very happy with himself. It seemed that finally the world was on his side for a change. Nothing could bring him down on a day like this, he thought.

He drove down the bumpy dirt road until the large mansion appeared on top of the hill on the right hand side. Reaching the end of the road he pulled into the winding bitumen driveway that meandered towards the house. Dave admired the manicured gardens that extended into the

x

distance on both sides, the trees now blooming with their spring growth and the mansion that filled the windshield in front of him was pure magnificence.

The house itself was a triple storey with a four-berth garage attached to the left-hand side. It was a double-brick construction dominated by the French windows and a large pair of Corinthian columns on either side of the entrance that supported the terrace area above. Between these columns was a sweeping staircase carved from the finest rose coloured granite. Truly, this was a magnificent building and the views from the upper level were exquisite.

Dave pulled the ute up at the base of the staircase, got out and started up the steps.

'Get off those frigging clean steps!' came a wild high-pitched scream from inside the house.

Dave jumped back in alarm 'Aww, come on Mum, why can't I come in? I mean it is my house!' he yelled back.

'Jezuz, Dave, I may be your mother but someone's gotta tell ya that you stink like one of those chemical toilets on a 40 degree day,' answered his Mum. 'So get outta here and go round the back.'

Dave slumped down and headed back towards the ute. 'Hey, Dave!' called his Mum. Dave looked up, hopeful of a change of heart.

His Mum continued, 'Is that a bloody earring you've got on? All these years of looking after ya and I've raised a pansy,' she moaned and slammed the front door.

Dave reached up and pulled off the clip on earring. 'Oh well,' he muttered, 'it was worth a try.' Feeling very dejected, he went back to the ute. He got in and looked out of the window longingly. 'Hmmph, it's my house and I should be allowed to live in it.'

Dave cast his mind back to the time when it was only him in the house. The garbage had been piled everywhere and what were now lawns had been basically just a paddock. For six years he'd lived in a small shack out the back whilst he'd built this place using the finest items deposited in the dump. When it was complete he had enjoyed a year of the luxurious life but then Mother had come to visit. Mother was probably not the right title for her although it was biologically correct. Medusa may have been more appropriate as she turned most to stone with a single glance. Cerberus, the three-headed dog that guarded the gates of hell, could have been a good comparison. Then again the Widowmaker may have been even more apt, as she had been through nine husbands, all of which had died. Not necessarily due to a lack of care but more likely that after living with her for a while they simply seemed to want to die. It was a feeling Dave was beginning to understand all too well.

She had screamed and yelled and sent him back to his shack whilst she got things at the house 'in order'. That was five years ago now and she was still here and showed no signs of wanting to move on despite the regular collection of retirement home brochures Dave sent to her. He had even tried the old 'You've won a holiday' prank call routine on her to try and get her out of the house but she had spotted it as a fake straight away. It probably had something to do with the fact that Dave had used Afghanistan as the destination.

It was a somewhat deflated Dave that set off around the back of the mansion to the small shack that was hidden from view in the shadow of the building. This was a small area that still reflected Dave's glory days when garbage was king. Mum had been here too and tried to fix it with potted roses and herb gardens, all of which, fortunately, had failed.

Dave parked the ute on top of the patch of heavily oil-contaminated ground. Hard to believe that so much oil could come from one car but it had. That reminded Dave that he did need to top up the twenty-litre drum in the back, which he had connected to the engine to ensure that he wouldn't run out at an inopportune time, again.

The shack was one of those portable offices and much the same as the one at the dump but at least this one had a bed. Dave had got out of the ute and started to get his things from the back when a can of dog food smashed into the back of his head. Everything went dark for a few seconds but he was roused by his Mum's voice.

'And don't forget to feed the dogs,' she called down from the kitchen on the second floor.

Dave rubbed his head and turned to face the window but it had already closed. He thought about pitching the can back where it had come from but he knew that such an action would simply make her even madder and Mum in a bad mood was not a pleasant thing to experience. It was simply one of those unwritten rules in life, things that everyone knew you didn't do like asking Superman why his undies were on the outside of his trousers or kneeing a SAS solider in the nuts. You simply did not make Mum mad because it was too frightening and dangerous for all involved. So, swearing to himself, he made off to the shack, can of dog food in hand, to settle in for a quiet evening.

The interior of the shack was quite pleasant, from a rat's perspective. The furniture was of higher quality than that at the dump and being removed from the source of most of the parasites it lasted at least twice as long. Dave had even been selective about the pictures he had sticky taped to the wall. There was a mixture of landscapes, portraits, nudes, cars and a calender from the pig farmers association.

Dave gazed longingly at the calendar, musing yet again about the sender. It had been a present from a close friend. A lovely girl, she was the daughter of one of the local pig farmers. Totally devoted to her animals, she spent many hours with her favourite pigs. She was the type who didn't bother with gumboots when you had to wade out into the middle of the pigpen to catch up with a rutting sow or a runaway piglet. And the smell, yes, she was a girl who had her own special bouquet, one not dissimilar to Dave's own.

Her name was Caroline Grace Margaret Postlethwaite, named by her mother after her three favourite princesses. Her mother ignored all the signs of a child that was obviously going to be large; she'd been the tallest in her class, with a shoe size three fittings larger than everyone else, but she insisted on sending her to ballet school. Despite her mother's best wishes and hopes she kept on growing, culminating in her size 18 stature, which Dave classed as both meaty and fulfilling. She had been her mother's pride and joy. Unfortunately her mother had met an untimely demise by falling into a yard full of hungry piglets. They were all desperately hungry and they had sucked every inch of her body in search of milk. The resulting 'love bites' and bruising from eager snouts had drained her body's blood supply and she had perished three days later. Caroline's father had never recovered.

Dave and Caroline had always had an on and off affair. Dave would have liked a lot more of the 'on' but then again it probably would have killed him. She had proven to be a very energetic girl with incredible stamina. Oh the places they had been, the pigpen, the smokehouse, the piglet nursery and the slaughterhouse. Although Dave still had some disturbing dreams about that one as she had been very excited and enthusiastic in that location.

It had been an illicit affair; indeed it had to be because her father was almost an exact compliment to Dave's mother. If he had caught Dave with his daughter he would have grabbed a boning knife and it would have been sausage and meatballs for tea. What's more the bastard would have savoured every mouthful and obviously it would be the last time Dave ever tried makin' bacon.

Still that calender had brought back so many memories, and urges, most of which were pleasant and made him think that maybe it was time to pursue that relationship again. Yes, maybe once Henri had paid up it might be time to invite her on a luxurious holiday somewhere away from both their parents.

Dave walked up to the microwave and looked at the meal his mother had left in the fridge for him. Some sort of sludge and three veg, looking a bit like tuna casserole, he considered, but with his Mum's cooking you could never be sure. He put it in the oven and pressed the 'start' button. Then grabbed the can opener and opened the tin of dog food and dropped it into the dog's bowl. The microwave chimed and Dave removed the concoction. The aroma was disgusting even to Dave.

He considered his options and then took the plate out and dropped it at the door. 'Here boy,' he called, and promptly turned away and headed back inside before the dog could have a chance to bite him. He then settled down to a nice bowl of Pal, which he thoroughly enjoyed, especially the marrowbone jelly.

Dave relaxed and watched the television for a while, channel surfing the whole time. This had actually been the attraction of this particular TV because the channel selection board was damaged causing it to constantly rotate through all the channels with a 5-second pause on each. If you wanted to watch one program then you had to mash the remote continuously to get it to stay in one spot. So he settled down to watch the news, comedy, SBS movie and sports reviews. He waited until the good bits came up on SBS and then mashed the remote and watched intently. When that bit finished he smiled and headed off to bed looking forward to a just, although indecent, reward for his day's work. However, sleep just wouldn't come easily, as somehow he couldn't get the idea of Caroline out of his head. He tried counting sheep but instead found them turning into pigs cheekily swinging their buttocks as they jumped the fence. Others just seemed to wallow on their backs suggestively.

Sweating, he sat bolt upright. 'God,' he said, 'if pigs are becoming attractive perhaps it's time to go and risk it all again'. His mind made up, he reached under the bed and pulled out the package he had kept there for times like these and tucked it under his arm. Quickly he got dressed and then moved out to the ute, dodging the dog as it leaned out from its basket trying hard to sink its teeth into his calf, and jumped into the ute.

As he got into the driver's seat he recoiled as he found the reward the dog had left for him in exchange for such a fine meal. 'Hmm, perhaps I should have shared the Pal,' he thought whilst carefully removing it from the seat. But nothing, not even this, was now going to distract him from his wanton desires. He started the vehicle and headed out along the driveway and onto the country roads.

It was a fairly uneventful trip. Sure there had

been the usual suicidal wombats, kangaroos and a strange striped dog with a kangaroo like tail but he'd managed to miss them all whilst only making minor modifications to the car. As he neared Caroline's place he knew he would have to take more care. About two kilometres out he turned off the lights and made his way forward by the light of the moon that was slowly climbing in the sky. Unfortunately Dave's eyesight was less than ideal under perfect conditions and when driving by moonlight he careered from side to side as he reacted to the items that he could identify. However after a number of close calls he finally pulled up at the entrance to Caroline's place.

The sign over the entrance read Hog Warts and as far as Dave was concerned it was a magical place where he had certainly been taught a few lessons. He parked the ute to one side of the driveway, grabbed the parcel, and keeping low, headed along the fence towards the house. He paused as one of the dogs noticed him and started barking but after a few token protests it stopped and Dave continued on his way.

Keeping low he reached the pigpen that was placed at the front of the yard and then implemented the next stage of his plan. Opening the parcel he revealed a bright pink pig suit. Dave sighed, 'The things we do for lust,' he muttered and pulled the suit on. He then jumped the fence into the pigpen, dropped onto all fours and started making loud 'oinking' noises.

Now any good farmer is tuned to the sounds of their animals and it was obvious to any pig farmer that this one was in distress, otherwise why would it sound so bad? Dave knew that Caroline was definitely tuned into her pigs and would soon respond. And indeed there was soon a blaze of lights from the house. Dave heard the door open and he waited to hear her dulcet tones.

'What's the matter with you, pig?' came a gruff, male voice.

Dave froze. This wasn't Caroline, it was her father! He kept down on all fours and slowly turned his head towards the voice. Shit! It was him! What to do?

Caroline's father studied the pig with interest, although without his glasses, that he had forgotten in his hurry to help the animal, he could not make out the fine details. 'You're a pretty looking pig, aren't you?' he said as he opened the gate and started towards Dave.

Dave backed off until he felt his butt hit the corner of the pen. There was nowhere else to go. But if he revealed himself the old bastard would kill him, but if he didn't then he'd.... Well it didn't bear thinking about; what a choice!

Whilst Dave was deliberating, Caroline's father kept advancing towards him saying things like 'Who's a pretty pig, then?' and 'Don't be afraid of Daddy'. Despite this encouragement Dave was seriously afraid and his nemesis was getting very close.

Caroline's father was about to reach down and grab this pig by the snout when he heard another voice. 'I'll take care of this one, Dad, it's a little strange and needs special care,' said Caroline in a no nonsense tone.

Dave just about fainted on hearing her voice. He was saved! If she hadn't turned up then it was quite likely that he and the old man could have been engaged or at least they would have moved their relationship to a new plane.

Her father hesitated but he couldn't see a way to argue so he shrugged, 'OK, Dear, you take care of it,' he said with some disappointment and turned and walked back to the house.

Caroline knelt down beside Dave. 'That was close,' she said, 'I thought you were going to be tomorrow's main course'. Dave just shivered. They both waited in silence until the door shut and the lights in Dad's bedroom were turned off.

Dave sat up, glad to be off all fours, 'Jesus, I came her to see you and that bastard nearly had me. If you hadn't turned up I reckon I'd have been porked.'

Caroline laughed, 'No way, I was here all the time and I was just letting you sweat a bit. I mean it has been a while since you came to see me hasn't it?'

Dave mumbled something about being busy and overseas whilst Caroline smirked, enjoying seeing Dave squirm trying to justify his absence. 'OK that's enough' she said. 'So what have you been doing today.'

Dave looked up grateful to be on a safer topic. 'Oh I was out in the bay dodging submarines and protestors.'

Caroline came him a penetrating stare. 'And why did you come here? To see my father? Or perhaps it was to play submarines out here was it?'

Dave was feeling a little more confident. 'Well submarines sounds OK to me.'

Caroline smiled and moved closer. 'And what did you imagine, open the hatches and launch torpedoes eh?'

'Well even getting to periscope depth sounded pretty good to me,' said Dave smirking.

For the next couple of hours till dawn the nighttime stillness was broken by strange animal sounds and the occasional call of 'Dive, dive, dive'.

chapter 08

Back in the comparative comfort of his office, Dave relaxed. He was feeling a little tired this morning and had strained quite a few muscles the previous night, especially the one at the back of his tongue. Still it was worth it. Now all he needed was for Henri to cough up with the dough and then he could take Caroline on an all expenses paid trip. Dave hadn't quite made up his mind about where to go. The Leongatha Daffodil Festival seemed appropriate. As far as Dave was concerned he didn't want to go anywhere that would give Caroline a reason to leave the hotel room. But then again the last overseas trip had proven an unexpected bonus and so it may be worth spending the cash after all, he considered. Thinking of that trip reminded him of the business at hand.

Dave reached for his mobile and punched in the long series of numbers needed to reach a certain residence in Paris. After a lot of ringing a sleepy voice answered the phone, 'Oui.'

'Henri, is that you? Where the hell's my cash?'

'Dave? Is zat you? You're still alive!' exclaimed Henri.

'Course I'm a bloody live. Now if you'll cough up with the cash I can get on with living!' screamed Dave.

'Dave, do not be like zat. I have arranged with some friends who will pay you off personally.'

'When?' quizzed Dave.

'Err, I do not know zat. Perhaps this week,' continued Henri.

Dave was by now getting very hot under the collar. 'You're not going to pay me are you, you bastard?' yelled Dave, his face turning redder with each passage of conversation.

Henri was squirming, 'Zat is a harsh way to put it, Dave,' he paused and then considered that this fool would not be around for much longer, 'but it is correct. I will not be paying. Au revoir,' he stated calmly and then he hung up.

'Mongrel, froggy bastard! French prick!' ranted Dave throwing the phone against the back wall of the office. 'If I could get my hands on that prick I'd wring his scrawny neck, I'd plant a size ten fair up his clacker! What else can you expect from a race that reckons frogs and snails are good tucker!'

Dave continued in this manner for a number of hours, incredibly never once repeating a curse.

Finally the dump resounded to, 'and may your chooks turn into emus and kick ya dunny down!' and Dave, exhausted, collapsed into his chair. This had by now started to deteriorate from the numerous other members of the dump that had come to infest this prize piece of real estate.

Slim had been cowering in the shed, but emerged when the sounds of silence finally came to the dump and he apprehensively moved to the office. Opening the door he saw Dave resting in the chair. This was far better than last time when Dave had instead been hiding behind the door with a cricket bat waiting for a chance to vent that last bit of frustration.

'Er, got a problem Dave?' asked Slim cautiously.

'That mongrel, slimy, wart covered, frog bastard,' muttered Dave.

Slim, still not sure what that implied, asked, 'What did he do?'

'Bastard won't pay!' yelled Dave. 'I go out on the bay, freeze my balls off, tackle a warship, play tootsie with a heap of greenies and all for nothing! Not a frigging cent, or for that matter a Euro.' He paused, 'Jeez if I had him and a blunt knife I'd really 'steel' a moment with his nuts.'

Slim decided that it would be best to depart rapidly before Dave saw him as a potential substitute for Henri.

Dave slumped back into the chair, disrupting at least three colonies of fleas.

'Bastard,' he muttered again. So here he was, all that work had been for nothing. His dump was still filling up and no alternatives had been found. So, back to square one with nothing to show for it.

'Now what? No way can I go them frigging worms.' He was still haunted by the sight of Jacques and those thousands of worms crawling from every part of his body. He shivered at the memory, but what other choice was there? Christ, that friggin' frog was gonna turn him 'green' but there seemed to be no alternative. His shoulders slumped with that total resignation usually reserved for prisoners on Death Row.

With deep regret, Dave went outside and surveyed the dump for something useful. Finding an old water tank with a rusted out bottom he decided to use that as temporary worm farm. But where to put it? He looked around again. The most obvious spot was where Slim had buried those boxes; at least there the ground was still soft. So he dragged the tank over to that spot and dropped it into place.

With that done he jumped into the front-end loader and picked up a pile of compost, or rather something that would eventually be classed as compost, and filled the tank.

'Now all I need is some worms,' said Dave. He put the bucket down and scraped the surface but the worms that he pulled out were terrible specimens. Even the fish that John West reject wouldn't have touched them.

Dave sighed, 'Guess I'll have to buy some of the long, skinny, mongrel bastards,' he said and moved towards the old ute. He clambered in and set off for his local garden centre, 'Green Thumbs R Us'.

God, he hated that place. Everything was always stored in neat compartments, there were flowers everywhere, whimsical concrete statues, and oh-so-neat paving. Even the machinery was washed and sparkling. If Dave's dump was heaven, that place was hell, as far as he was concerned.

He pulled up outside the main entrance, blue smoke belching from his vehicle, and immediately one of the assistants ran towards him.

'Can I park your car for you, Sir?' he asked. Dave grudgingly passed him the keys and headed towards the office thinking all the time that this must be another of those queer ideas that they got from the Yanks. What he didn't realise was that the service was only provided to him in the interests of not scaring off the other customers. Also the poor assistant, who would not be fit to work for the next three days, was only doing this for the danger money that was paid to him by the boss and all the other workers.

Jim, the owner, rushed outside to greet him. As with most gardeners, strong smells had little effect on him. 'Dave, long time no see. Come with me round the back, we've got three new types of manure that may interest you,' he said.

Long time no see, huh, not bloody long enough, thought Dave. 'Cut the crap Jim, all I want is worms.'

'Going fishing are we?'

'Nah I'm going to make some compost,' answered Dave.

Jim was shocked. 'Dave, er, you're not going green on me are you?'

'Don't say that G-word near me, you bastard. Just sell me a bag of worms and then I can get out of here,' said Dave.

Jim turned, 'Sure, Dave, just follow me.'

Dave trudged along behind Jim as he led him

on a roundabout path to the sheds at the back of the garden centre. Jim opened the door and moved towards a number of small tanks.

'What sort did you want Dave?' he asked.

'Squiggly ones,' Dave answered sarcastically.

'No,' said Jim, 'there are many different types, do you know what type you want?'

Well up to now the only two types of worms that Dave had noticed was the cooked variety on a footpath and the live type in the ground. Oh and an in-between class which included those placed on a fishing hook. But Jim with the infinite patience that one comes to expect from a garden centre owner went on to explain.

'There's these little guys,' Jim said, putting his hand deep into the first tank, 'these are red tigers.' He pulled a handful out, Dave was instantly reminded of Jacques but he managed to hide his distaste. Jim went on blissfully, 'You can tell them as each segment is clearly defined by a yellow band. They are similar to a Red in that their clitellum is raised, commencing at segment 32 and going up to and including segment 34. Tigers have an in-built defence mechanism; when they are threatened, like someone trying to put them on a fishing hook, they exude a fetid, unpleasant-smelling yellow liquid.' He dived into another bin. 'Over here we have Reds, a European worm, deep red in colour. They grow to about seventy five millimetres, when placed in soil they will always be found in the top 150 millimetres.' He headed to another bucket.

'These are Blues, and they come in four different colours at sexual maturity and they can add a fifth as they approach their full body size. Once Blues reach a length of about seventy millimetres they begin to phosphoresce a deep blue/purple on exposure to light. As the size increases so does the degree of phosphorescence and at full size they will flash a regal purple. When put in the light they will whip into a U shape and constantly reverse this position. They whip about so vigorously that they can snap themselves in half.'

Dave by now was just sick of worms. 'Just give me a bag of them first ones, pink pussies, or whatever you called them,' said Dave.

'Red Tigers,' corrected Jim patiently as he reached for a bag and filled it with a couple of kilograms of the worms. 'Here you go, Dave they should work a treat. Look forward to seeing some of your compost soon,' said Jim.

Dave took the bag, handed over some cash and slunk away. 'I'd like to give him some of my compost now, yeah, fresh before it's had time to mulch,' muttered Dave as he headed to the car park. As he emerged, his car swung round from its hiding spot at the back. The attendant leaped from the car whilst both holding the door open and his lunch in. Dave climbed in and sped away, glad to escape from such a horrible, pristine, sterile environment.

Back at the dump he walked out to his new worm farm tank and up-ended the bag, releasing the worms inside it. 'Red tigers, huh?' he thought. Most of them just stayed curled up in ball, however one started to burrow into the ground. 'Go on, Red,' he yelled, 'at least one of ya has got some guts.' In disgust he walked back to the shed, gathered his things and called it a day.

* * *

The next day was dark and miserable, matching Dave's mood perfectly.

On arriving at his dump the first thing he did was to head out to the tank and check on his worms. There they were, still curled up in a ball but now all were as stiff as maggots, dead, deceased, with us no more, cactus, gone, passed away.

All but one which popped its head out when it felt Dave's presence. It was almost as if it recognised Dave and it emitted a foul yellow liquid as a greeting. 'Well at least you've got some guts, Red,' muttered Dave as he turned away in disgust.

'Bloody worms,' he sighed and feeling even more depressed retreated to the shed to think up a new scheme.

chapter 09

HENRI HAD ALWAYS BEEN ONE TO TURN ADVERSITY into opportunity and this had been a very good time for that indeed. First he had been able to dispose of fifty kilograms of plutonium at no cost other than an upset Australian. Now he had avoided the grasp of the worlds two foremost terrorists who would remove that Australian and then most likely commit suicide in a major terrorist attack, destroying the plutonium and God alone knows what else along with all connections to himself.

No one would be left alive who knew that he had ever been involved. But just to be sure…

Henri picked up the phone and dialled the headquarters of the Israeli intelligence agency, Mossad. "Ello,' he said, 'I zink you should know that two international terrorists will be boarding a plane to Australia zoon,' and then he hung up.

He leaned back in his chair and smiled. If they did not take care of themselves in their attack then surely Mossad would finish off the job.

Mossad did indeed take the call seriously and started to monitor and observe many of the flights from Europe to Asia and Australia. After a couple of weeks the waiting proved worthwhile as the cross referencing of all bookings identified that there were two false identities being used on one particular flight.

Mossad however were not happy to stop there. Henri's call had also been traced and a detailed dossier on him and his history was also being prepared.

Therefore it was not surprising that a week later Henri had an unexpected visitor. This tall, dark and obviously very fit, thirty-something man introduced himself as Uri and suggested that they adjourn to Henri's office to discuss 'business'.

Henri was unsure about this visitor. He had a demeanour that suggested that he was not here for Henri's usual type of business. But what? Henri sat down behind his desk and Uri moved to the visitor's chair in front of him.

'Zo,' said Henri, 'what can I do for you?'

Uri smiled, 'My organisation would like a little more information and we believe that you could assist us.' He didn't elaborate on what his organisation was; but then again he did not need to. Henri understood perfectly.

'Oh,' said Henri, 'and what could I do for you. I mean I am but a humble proprietor of this rubbish dump?'

Uri leaned across the desk. 'No, Henri,' he smiled 'we know who and what you are and we know the people that are looking for you. Now,' he continued, 'we can come to an amicable arrangement or I can walk away from here and pass your details on to the French Foreign Legion.' Henri looked shocked. Uri kept the pressure on. 'Yes, Henri, we know about your colleagues and I am sure that they would love to have you back with them in central Africa, especially the ones you left to die when you deserted after they sent you to get reinforcements.'

Henri had gone from white to yellow to whiter than white. He knew that a return to the Legion would mean at the best a slow, cruel death and there were many who would want to deny him death's release. But what to do? If he admitted that he had been dealing in plutonium then there would be a queue of countries waiting to execute him. He slumped, it was a no win situation.

'Alright, Uri, what is it you want to know?' asked a very dejected Henri.

Uri smiled to himself and leaned back in the chair, this was much better. 'A week ago you made a call to our office and advised us that some terrorists would be boarding a plane to Australia. I want to know who, why and what they are planning to do.'

Henri drew even further back, he was probably going to die no matter what, but the survival instincts ran deep and so he decided to roll the dice one more time.

'Uri,' he started, 'there are two terrorists, Achmed and Yousef, whom I am sure you know and they are trying to catch up with a man called Dave. Yes,' continued Henri, 'Dave is the man you're looking for. He is working on a scheme so terrible and a weapon so inconceivable that he is attracting the interest of all the major terrorists in the world.' He leaned over the desk towards Uri and whispered, 'I can tell you where to find this man, he has a secret base in Australia with a very cunning disguise. For a fee of course.'

Uri leaned across the desk, 'Yes my friend I am happy to pay a fee. Shall we make it a small price, say, your life?'

'What do you mean?' spluttered Henri.

Uri smiled that calculating smile, 'I mean that you shall tell me all that you know and if it is of some significance then I shall let you continue to live,' explained Uri.

'You wouldn't,' blurted Henri already knowing that this man indeed would. Uri just continued to smile.

'Alright, alright,' said Henri, 'I am told that Achmed and Yousef are planning to steal this weapon of mass destruction, one that could destroy any major city and that they intend to use it on a suicide mission.'

Uri's face had hardened and he gave Henri a piercing gaze. 'What type of weapon are we talking about?' he asked. 'Conventional explosive, biological, chemical or perhaps nuclear?'

Henri shuddered at that last word. 'I do not know!' he yelled, 'they simply said that using this weapon would write their names in the stars.'

Uri realised that he would get nothing more from Henri. 'Alright,' he said, 'that is enough. Write me details of this Dave and I shall find him and his weapons before these filth can destroy millions of innocent people.' With that he turned and left, leaving Henri feeling relieved that he was still alive and had not been directly implicated in the supply of plutonium.

chapter (10)

ACHMED AND YOUSEF BOARDED THE PLANE with great trepidation. They had chosen their flight with great care, because they knew every terrorist in the world and their likely targets.

So there was no way that they would fly with an American company as they were obvious targets for Afghani, Palestinian, Iranian and Iraqi terrorists.

Air France was out as most countries in the world had a grudge against them.

The Irish were always likely to target British Airways.

Aeroflot just fell out of the sky without the assistance of explosives.

With Lufthansa, there was always someone who would remember the war.

In the end the only safe option seemed to be with the Australian airline Qantas. It seemed that they were only likely to be targeted by wild-life organisations against kangaroo culling. Still, you never knew when a random act of terrorism would occur. But given that these two were the major causes of those random acts they decided that the risk was low enough to take.

The flight was uneventful and they flew peacefully over Europe and landed for a stopover in Singapore. Here some passengers disembarked and others boarded. Achmed and Yousef watched them all pass by with a profes-sional interest but none registered as a threat. They were comfortable as the plane took off for the final seven-hour leg of the journey.

Unfortunately, mid way over the Timor Sea a group of three men, also of Middle Eastern appearance, jumped up and ran towards the cockpit. 'Do not move!' screamed the leader, 'we are taking over this plane and we will use it in our ultimate protest.'

Yousef and Achmed looked at each other and sighed. It was always painful to watch such amateurs at work. Much like a professional Shakespearian actor having to watch a children's primary school play.

The other travellers were starting to panic. The stewardess was screaming and children were crying. A Sky Marshal had stood up and drawn a gun and was slowly moving down the aisle towards where Achmed was seated.

Achmed had seen enough and he unbuckled his seat belt and stood up.

'Sit down!' yelled both the hijackers and the Marshal.

But Achmed just ignored them. He moved to the aisle, turned to the Marshal and said, 'Go to your seat and leave this to me.' The Marshal, stunned, froze where he was and awaited the outcome of the confrontation.

Achmed advanced towards the first of the hijackers. 'Who is your leader?' he asked. The hijacker nodded towards his colleague at the cabin entrance. 'Take me to him,' ordered Achmed in a tone that would not tolerate any questioning. Confused by this turn of events, the hijacker complied with the request and fell in behind Achmed as he moved to the front of the cabin.

The leader studied this man moving towards him. He was puzzled, as if he should recognise this person. Achmed reached a point just in front of the leader and stopped. 'Do you know me?' he asked.

The leader contemplated some more, 'You seem familiar but I cannot place you?' he answered.

Achmed switched to Arabic, 'Come closer and I will tell you who I am and what I will have done to you and your family if you do not do as I say.'

The leader and Achmed both leaned forward and Achmed started whispering to him. The second hijacker could only hear short snippets of the exchange, things like 'Fool, do you not recognise me, I am Achmed... My friend over there is Yousef... You will do as I say or... your testicles and those of your sons... camels will gorge themselves on your... four generations will pay for... Your eternal reward will be very short as I...

This continued for about five minutes throughout which time the leader continued to lose colour from his face as Achmed explained in great detail the atrocities that would be perpetrated on him, his family and extended family for many years to come if he did not comply with his wishes. Achmed stopped whispering into his ear and stood up, turned and headed back to his seat. The leader, now a deathly pale white called his two accomplices to his side where he explained the situation, occasionally pointing to where Yousef and Achmed sat impassively.

Eventually they stood up and moved towards the Sky Marshal. 'Excuse me, Sir,' started the leader, 'would you please be so kind as to forgive us our little joke. We will just take our seats now. Oh and here are our guns and knives. Have a nice day.' And with that they returned to their seats.

The Marshal was totally confused and his gaze flickered from Achmed to the hijackers. Finally he moved up to Achmed and demanded, 'What did you say to them?'

Slowly Achmed turned his gaze to the Marshal and said, 'I explained to them that due to the time difference this was now the sabbath day and that hijacking a plane on this particular Moslem holy day was against the teachings of Islam. I also pointed out that if they persisted their sacrifice would be for nothing as they and their families shall be cursed for generations to come.' With that he turned his gaze back to the front of the plane.

The Marshal, still reeling stammered, 'Oh, er, thank you, ah, Father. You will be well rewarded for your bravery.'

'No, no-one must know of my part in this or my own family could be targeted. I want you to take all of the credit,' Ahmed offered.

'Well, if you insist, Sir,' the Marshall happily agreed, and headed back towards the rear of the plane where he could safely lock away the weapons.

chapter 11

Dave, BLISSFULLY UNAWARE THAT HE WAS THE centre of a number of fates that were about to collide, relaxed in his chair and continued to contemplate the idea of mechanical worms.

This idea still appealed to him because at least a metal bastard wouldn't curl up and die in the sun. Plus it wouldn't run away when there was an electrical storm. Yes, this had to be the way to go.

He leaned back in his chair and looked out over the dump. A number of small accidents had occurred as people rushed to get in and get out whilst taking the minimum number of breaths possible. Funny how a lack of oxygen to the brain can affect their judgement when trying to make a hasty exit, particularly with a trailer attached to the car.

The dump resounded as normal with the sounds of heavy machinery, the crunch of metal, people yelling at each other, the buzzing of flies and the squawking of birds, usually either crows or ibis.

Crows were cunning mongrels, very hard to trick or catch. Ibis, well they are pretty dumb even for a bird and their stomachs rule their heads. Offer an ibis a free feed and it's pretty easy to get a free feed in return. Quite tasty when roasted but the flavour was definitely affected by the area of the dump that they had been eating. So far the general consensus was that garbage scraps ibis were better than household rubbish ibis, definitely the worst were the night shift sludge feeders. Not quite sure what it was that they fed on but they would hop around on one foot with a cross eyed look staring into space, sometimes they would look intently to the horizon whilst standing on one foot and then just fall to the side, stiff as a board. Somehow no matter how you cooked these they just didn't taste right.

Dave decided that he'd better start having

114

a look around for things that could be used as part of a mechanical worm.

Dave knew that it was going to be impossible to build an actual worm, therefore what he would have to do is to break down its functions into simple mechanisms. Not that there are many functions in a worm. The main thing it does is chew the stuff up at one end and shit it out the other, turning it a few times in the middle. Sounds simple enough but it had to be capable of chewing up anything. Worms are a little selective about what they eat, they won't chew on glass, shoes, engine blocks, cans or anything else other than basically food scraps. As a matter of fact they much preferred pre-digested food scraps. In other words it's not so much that they like something to eat as that they prefer to eat what someone else has already eaten.

Unfortunately most of what goes in a dump is not pre-digested so this thing would have to be big and tough and able to chew up anything that came its way. So metal would be the go. He cast his eye around. There was the old tractor with a broken axle that could be used for an engine, and a couple of pipes that could be used to make some sort of a grinder. Dave continued to eye everything, looking for anything that could possibly be used. After a few days he had an interesting pile of parts and he dragged these bits into the shed and set to work.

Eventually the contraption emerged, and it was amazing. Somehow it seemed to vaguely resemble a crop harvester without all the whirling bits up the front. It consisted of a large open chamber at the front so that the rubbish could go in and then pass through. Inside the chamber were a couple of pipes which had numerous teeth welded to them. The idea was that these would spin furiously, whacking everything that went through into a chewed up mass. These pipes were hooked to the old tractor motor by a large collection of v-belts. On each side a large tractor wheel was attached to hydraulic motors and at the rear there were two big castors.

On top of the chamber Dave had built a rudimentary cabin. It consisted of a seat and steering wheel from an old FJ Holden, a piece of rope for a seat belt, two large levers to activate the drives and the rotors and an assortment of switches. It was truly a unique piece of engineering, not that any engineer would want to claim responsibility for this device.

As would be expected, Dave's dedication to detail shone through in every aspect of its construction. When it came time to test the machine there was only one thing to do. 'Slim!' he roared.

Slim poked his head out from behind a pile of rubbish he was digging through 'Yep,' he answered.

Dave smiled. 'Come here, mate, I've got a small job for you.'

Slim, completely unaware that he was about to take on a job with a life expectancy comparable to that of a South American soccer player who had scored an own-goal in the World Cup, wandered over innocently.

'Just climb up there and kick it in the guts will you mate?' said Dave.

Slim clambered up to the top deck and Dave made a mental note that he should add some stairs before he tried it himself. Settling down into the seat he called back to Dave, 'What do I do now, Dave?'

Dave moved toward a large pillar and stepping behind it called, 'Just turn the key mate.'

Slim reached down, by now feeling a little apprehensive about the way Dave was cowering behind the largest shelter he could find, and turned the key. The engine behind him roared into life and then settled down to a steady idle. Dave paused to make sure that there was no chance of an explosion and then stepped out. 'OK, Slim, move the lever on your left forward. Oh, and you better put on the seat belt.' Slim reached down and tied the ropes in a granny knot around his middle. Then gritting his teeth he pushed the lever forward.

chapter 12

YOUSEF BREATHED A SIGH OF RELIEF AS THE plane touched down at the airport. He'd held his breath all the way; fearing that someone may have planted a bomb set to detect the rapid change in altitude, or maybe the impact of the landing. Indeed the captain had landed the plane so hard that for a moment he wondered if they had been shot down.

Achmed was also aware of all the usual triggering points for a bomb and had sat white-knuckled, gripping the seat with all his strength whilst a little old lady in the next seat tried her best to counsel him not to be afraid of flying.

The plane taxied slowly towards the terminal and when it arrived the passengers moved slowly to gather their hand luggage ready for their exit. Achmed and Yousef both waited for this initial rush to die down knowing that they had less chance of being detected if they were in the middle of the queue rather than at the front.

Once half the passengers had left they gathered their belongings and started the slow walk to the exit of the plane.

The terminal was like any other, bright lights and sleepy people trying to carry numerous bulging suitcases moving their way forward towards a central point in what seemed an infinite line.

Achmed and Yousef paused to collect their baggage. They both prayed that the first suitcase would not create an issue by exploding, as it dropped from the elevator onto the carousel. There was no need to worry though as their cases were treated with the love and respect that is universal amongst airport and postal workers. Achmed considered the contents of his baggage as he moved to the front of the queue for customs inspection. There was nothing in there that could be considered offensive, well offensive to one of the world's foremost terrorists that is. However, there was still a remote possibility that this customs officer could take offence at some of the material contained within.

A rather bored Customs Officer asked, 'Do you have anything to declare?' Never one to let an opportunity pass, Achmed said 'Yes! That the infidels have desecrated our lands and customs too much and now they must pay!'

The Customs Officer was jolted awake by this tirade and decided that he should take a little more interest in this one. 'I meant,' he asked intently, 'do you have anything illegal in your suitcase?'

'Illegal! ILLEGAL!' cried Achmed, 'Of course not. There is nothing in my suitcase that could be considered illegal; everything in there I carry all the time.' He looked at the Officer, 'Are you persecuting me because I am not like you?'

The Officer backed down bit after this outburst not wanting to risk facing discrimination charges. 'OK then,' he said with a steely gaze, 'let's take a look.'

The Customs Officer reached for the locks on the suitcase and Achmed froze. He knew that if those locks were pushed instead of slid that a set of throwing knives would be released from their hiding point behind the handle.

'Please be careful with the locks,' Achmed asked, 'they are old and need to be moved with care'. Surprised at the more compliant tone the Officer continued his inspection. He placed the case on the bench and slid the locks across. Achmed breathed a sigh of relief as the case opened without revealing the hidden compartment.

With the case open the Customs Officer commenced his routine search. The case was full of clothes, toiletries and the usual assorted items that a tourist would bring. Feeling along the base he noticed a small bump in the lining. 'What's this?' he asked and pushed it down. Achmed tried to look innocent and said 'Oh it's nothing, just a small stone trapped in the lining.' Meanwhile he tried to push the tray holding the various dismantled components of a 9mm pistol back into the base of the suitcase without disturbing the officer or the search.

But fortunately for Achmed something else had caught his eye. 'What's in this?' asked the Customs Officer holding up a shaving kit.

'Just a few personal items,' answered Achmed, squirming.

The officer opened the kit, 'Looks like some sharp objects that could be used as weapons. Hmm, I think I'll have to confiscate these,' he said.

Achmed looked worried, 'Could I at least keep the toothpaste, please?'

The Officer stared at him and his yellow, rotting teeth for what seemed an eternity. 'OK,' he said, 'but I'll keep the rest.' And so the tube of Semtex was returned to his suitcase and Achmed moved on to the outbound queue.

Yousef had at least learned from the experience.

'Do you have anything to declare?' asked the Customs Officer.

'I declare that Australia is a wonderful country and that its people are the most friendliest on earth,' said Yousef. The Customs Officer was a little taken aback by this answer and in shock passed him through with only a cursory glance.

Yousef leaned over to Achmed and said, 'My friend that was very close. It was only that fortune smiled that allowed you to proceed.'

Achmed, also shaken by this encounter replied, 'Yes, we must proceed with much more caution now. We were lucky this time but we must not make such a mistake again.' And thus the two of them moved to the exit, which led into the waiting terminal, greatly relieved to be off the plane and away from Customs.

'So now we need to find a way to get to this place,' said Yousef.

Achmed paused, 'Yes,' he agreed, 'but how? We will need personal transport as the railway and bus services are not as well developed as those at home.' Yousef looked at him in a strange way, as the only services he remembered were a cart that passed by about twice a day. Achmed continued, 'A vehicle, that is what we need!'

'Alright,' agreed Yousef, 'shall we steal one?'

Achmed considered this for a awhile 'No, we do not want to risk being discovered before we complete our mission. We will obtain one from a local agent.' With a flurry of robes they spun around and moved towards the hire car desks.

The people at the hire car desk were not sure what to make of these approaching characters. Could they be rich oil sheikhs? Perhaps they are just tourists? Or maybe they are businessmen? They didn't know. So they assumed the best, for them, and treated them as royalty.

'Greetings, Sahib,' said the salesman with a deep bow, 'how may we be of service?'

Achmed and Yousef were taken aback by this treatment, but loath to let an opportunity pass by, dived straight in.

Yousef waved his hand dismissively. 'We need transport, what can you provide?' The salesman stood up and looked these people up and down. 'Well Sirs, for people of your status we can provide a Rolls Royce limousine complete with driver,' he said.

They looked at each other. 'No, we need to conduct private business, therefore we will be driving ourselves.'

The salesman looked at these two again. 'Not sheikhs he thought, otherwise they would want a driver. Oh well, I'll lower the sights.'

He smiled. 'Could I interest you in a standard limousine then?'

Achmed considered this for some time and eventually he decided that a large car would be too conspicuous and they continued to haggle for an hour or so about the size of vehicle, type, manufacturer and cost until a suitable compromise was reached.

Finally it was a strange pair that boarded their brightly coloured scooters, one with a sidecar loaded with suitcases, and they rode away from the airport.

As strange as it may seem these disguises worked very well as most people were amused by the sight of the brightly coloured flowing robes standing out in the breeze. So much so that they laughed so hard that they could not remember any specific details about the pair. Achmed and Yousef worked their way through the city and out into the bush towards the resting-place of the material that would bring them greatness.

chapter 13

Slim pushed the lever forward and all hell broke loose.

The machine leaped forward with all the blades underneath whirling at an incredible speed. Slim held the wheel with strength born from sheer terror. It exited the shed and headed out into the dump proper.

'Turn the wheel!' yelled Dave.

But Slim didn't respond. Every muscle was locked and he knew that his only hope was to ride this thing until it stopped.

The machine was headed for the trench. Slim considered the fact that there was no roll-over protection system fitted and decided that some action was needed if he was to survive. He pulled on that wheel with all his might. At first it seemed that nothing was to come from his efforts and the machine ploughed on as the trailing wheels skidded across the muddy surface, but slowly it responded and began to move to the right.

'Not the bloody office!' screamed Dave as the machine hurtled towards his humble abode.

Slim also realised the threat that the machine posed to his collection of Playboy and Penthouse magazines that he had gathered over the years and with a superhuman effort he pulled it around to the left. The machine fought and bucked underneath him but slowly it turned.

However this put him on a collision course with the trench again. Rather than risk running over the edge he steered it towards the entrance to the trench. This resulted in something that is still talked about in every pub in town.

As the machine entered the trench the blades bit deep into the rubbish that had been dumped there. It quickly chewed it up and spat it out the back. In fact it threw a rooster tail of rubbish about twenty metres into the air before it collapsed back into a neat pile behind the machine. If it happened to come across something that it couldn't digest, such as an engine block, it simply picked it up and spat it out of the front of the machine. That was how Dave's ute was changed to a convertible.

Slim just hung on and watched the huge rooster tail of rubbish from the rear and the continuous launching of metal projectiles from the front of the machine. At least whilst it moved through the trench he didn't have to worry about trying to steer the damn thing, Slim thought. In fact, now that he didn't have to worry about controlling it, it wasn't a bad thing to play with after all. Unfortunately the trench was coming to an end.

The machine started the upward climb and as it was about to burst forth from the trench it let out a loud cough and stopped. Slim was almost cut in two by the rope as he was pulled to a sudden stop. Never one to look a gift horse in the mouth he untied the knot and dropped to the ground, running, and he didn't stop until he was clear of both the machine and the trench.

Dave ran over to him, weaving in and out of the stunned patrons who had stopped to stare in disbelief at the crazed antics of this lunatic and his machine. Slim just stood there staring at the machine, shaking and struggling to control various bodily functions.

'It bloody worked!' screamed Dave, grabbing Slim round the waist and swinging him around.

Slim gave up all hope of self-control and vomited, splattering many of those nearby. He also decorated Dave's shirt in a way well known to parents of babies, but Dave was too excited to notice.

'Look at that eh!' yelled Dave dropping Slim who was still trying to recover from his near death experience. 'Look,' he said pointing to the trench, 'one big bloody row of compost.'

Dave was right. The machine had chewed up all the garbage and melded it into one long stream of compost. All the metal objects had been thrown clear and it was indeed a wonder that no one had been decapitated. Mind you if anyone had been, as long as they fell into the trench there wouldn't have been much in the way of evidence. If at knock-off time there were still a car there without an owner he would investigate that possibility further.

'Dave?' asked Slim, finally regaining a semblance of control.

'Yeah, what mate?' replied Dave.

Slim hesitated. 'Dave, why did it stop?' he asked.

'I thought you did it,' said Dave. 'But if you didn't then I guess it must have run out of fuel. I mean I couldn't find a decent tin so I used an old lawn mower fuel tank, only held about a litre.'

Slim hated to think what might have happened if Dave had been able to find a 20 litre drum. 'Er, Dave?' he began, choosing his words very carefully, 'I think it might need a little bit more work. Perhaps drop the engine revs a bit and maybe adjust the steering. Maybe give it a coat of paint?'

Dave wasn't impressed with the idea that his invention could be considered anything less than perfect. But the idea of it being finished with a bright coat of paint, especially caterpillar yellow, did have appeal.

'Alright, Slim,' he said, 'you can fix her up and give her a coat.' Dave wandered back to the office, past the punters who were still staring in disbelief at what they had seen. He was feeling very proud of his mechanical worm.

'Oh,' added Dave, 'while you're there push some of the compost into a heap over where the worms were.'

Slim was just pleased at having the opportunity to make some adjustments and modifications that might extend his life. So he wandered off to get a dozer to tow the beast back to the shed.

chapter 14

OVER THE NEXT FEW WEEKS THE DUMP changed forever, in much the same way as a caterpillar changes to a butterfly.

First the rotting piles of rubbish no longer gathered in festering cesspools of infection. Instead the machine processed everything with ruthless efficiency. With no rotting garbage the smell had gone and all the rubbish was being processed into compost that people would pay to take away. Some had even gone to the trouble of now sorting out their garbage to suit this new wonder of technology. This meant no more need to rat through all the garbage looking for the good bits, people just handed them to him on a plate. The people who came in were even using the box that Slim had set up at the entrance marked 'Playboy/Penthouse Recycling.'

Of course for Dave this was a far from ideal situation. His lifestyle was changing and now people even wanted to stop and chat with him when they dropped off their rubbish. This was something he wasn't used to. But on the positive side they weren't filling up his tip and there was money coming in from the garbage, the recyclers and the compost. It was a truly amazing situation. Even some people from the Australian Greenhouse Office had turned up and said that they would be arranging credits for all the greenhouse gases that he was not emitting from his tip.

Slim had bought a new pair of white overalls and after three weeks they were still recognisable as being white.

Slim had spent a lot of time getting the beast tidy. It now had a cabin and roll cage. It was finished in a lovely bright yellow coat of paint and Slim had rigged up a set of stairs leading to the cabin. It started, stopped and even steered in the directions that it was meant to. Slim even had a painting of a robot worm on each side.

Whenever it operated people would just

pause and watch as their rubbish was transformed into compost. Some would even break into spontaneous applause.

However, the ecological damage rort by these changes was immense, with many flies, fleas, rats, crows and ibis deprived of what had been their natural habitat. Instead they had moved into the nearby town in plague proportions, which had made many of the Christian fundamentalists believe that the great plagues of Egypt were again being wrought upon them, but this time all at once. With such dire proclamations of the coming apocalypse church attendances were higher than ever. Indeed due to the changes to Dave's tip this had indeed become a 'God-fearing' town.

Dave's tip had also risen in popularity and had become the star attraction for miles around. It had even reached a stage where other bludging bastards were coming to his tip on Government sponsored study tours. Some were even interested in buying his machine.

Even more amazing was the fact that his mother had now taken to asking him into the house for the occasional meal. This was a dramatic change, a whole new concept for Dave. He had never thought beyond just building a mechanical worm. Suddenly he was presented with other opportunities that he would never have considered. A franchise for Dave's Tip had become a possibility. Yeah he thought, I could have lots of guys running around with trailers that have Dave's Tip painted down the side, perhaps with my face on them with small mechanical worms inside.

Dave never considered the fact that using his face as advertising was unlikely to have beneficial effects for the business. Indeed it was quite likely to have the opposite effect.

Dave was blissfully reflecting on the possibility of bright yellow trailers cruising all parts of suburbia with his face glaring at all when a tall, dark stranger appeared. 'Are you the Manager of this establishment?' asked the stranger.

'Who wants to know?' challenged Dave, hoping that it wasn't another one of them EPA bastards.

The stranger put out his hand, 'My name is Uri and I have come from Israel to learn about this wonderful operation that you have here.'

Dave looked at him suspiciously but shook his hand anyway. 'My name's Dave and yeah, I'm in charge. So what is it that you want to know Uri, and why?' asked Dave.

Uri cleared a corner of the desk and sat down. 'Dave, my people have very little land and we need to recycle virtually everything that we can to ensure that we will survive. My government has asked me to come here and learn from you so that we can apply your techniques at home.'

Dave looked him up and down wondering why they had such a problem, I mean with all the bombs that went off you would think that one thing they were not short of was holes that you could fill. But never one to look a gift horse in the mouth he spoke up. 'So you're here bludging on the Israeli government, is that right?'

Uri squirmed. 'Well, Dave that is not the words that I would use but I guess you could put it that way.'

Dave's eyes light up. Now here was someone he could relate to. The only problem was how to turn this to his advantage. I mean Dave knew what was involved in these study tours and he knew that there was plenty of funding available, but how to tap into it was always the challenge.

'Well, Uri,' said Dave, 'If you want to learn the business there's only one way to do it, and that's to get your hands dirty. So I'll do you a deal. You work here and learn, but you'll have to pay me $1,000 a week plus all royalties due if you use the ideas back home.'

'But...' Uri paused. 'Dave, I must talk to my Government but I think it will be all right. I will have an answer for you tomorrow.' With that he turned and left.

Dave sat back and smiled. What a situation! If this worked then he could get all them bludging bastards working for him and be paid for the privilege. Wow, things just couldn't get any better.

Uri continued back to his car smiling to himself. Sure this was an unexpected increase in the cost of the mission but if successful the value to the free world would far exceed anything spent here. Still, there was the obligatory phone call to make. He paused and looked around. Oh well, he thought, looks like this will be home for awhile.

He cast his eyes around the rubble that formed the dump, the rotting shack, the crumbling machinery shed and waste up to his knees. 'Yes', he smiled, 'come to think of it, it will be a lot like living in downtown Beirut again.'

chapter

THE NEXT DAY URI ARRIVED FOR WORK AT THE dump. He was dressed in loose-fitting, fresh, white overalls and new, bright orange gumboots. Dave watched him approach and shook his head. 'Silly bastard will learn soon enough,' he chuckled.

'Hello, Dave,' Uri called. 'I am here to learn the business, and here is your first week's payment,' and he handed over a cheque to Dave.

'Can't argue about that,' Dave muttered. At least this was one foreigner who would pay his bills up front, he thought. Better than that froggy bastard, Henri, he thought and again many explicit images of Henri's orifices and various items of equipment crossed his mind. 'OK, Uri, follow me,' said Dave and he turned and headed off towards the main shed.

Uri followed behind him after adjusting the 9mm pistol that sat snuggled under the overalls near his left armpit. There was no way he was going to be unprepared for the likes of Achmed or Yousef when they turned up. But why would they have any interest in a place like this, he wondered. He looked around. There was only a couple of shacks, the main machinery shed and assorted piles of rotting garbage. Perhaps their interest is in Dave rather than anything here, but why? Could it be that Dave had once been a member of ASIO? Perhaps he had been a member of a counter terrorist organisation? But if so then why do we know nothing about him? Could he have been a member of an extreme Jewish group? Somehow none of these seemed possible but there had to be a reason why they would want to come here and he was determined to find out what it was.

Dave arrived at the main machinery shed and turned and waited while Uri sauntered up to him. 'Now, me boy,' he said, 'if you want to understand this game you've got to begin at the bottom and work your way up.' Dave patted the composter and turned to Uri, 'Therefore,' he said, 'you're first job will be to clean this baby down. That way you'll get to know her and when you understand her we might let you take her out.' Dave smirked thinking to himself that it would take at least six months of cleaning and general yard work before he'd let any other bastard on his machine.

'Hmm, six months free work and $1,000 a week, not bad, not bad at all,' he muttered once he'd walked away from Uri and the shed.

Uri grabbed the hose and started to wash down the machine. 'Could this be what they are after?' he wondered to himself. No, this was just a commercial machine, sure it could be used as a weapon to grind up anyone that got in front of it and that may make it popular for crowd/protestor control in a number of countries. Certainly the Police would have loved such a machine at the Anti Globalisation marches. The Tianenmen Square protest in China could also have been different if they had been driving this rather than a tank. But no international terrorist would be chasing such a machine as it was slow and could not do enough damage to highlight their cause.

He shrugged his shoulders and continued on his way, washing and then cleaning all parts of the machine, and closely inspecting each item for any alternative application such as hidden missile launchers. But nothing of interest could be found. He would have to spend more time looking elsewhere. In the meantime he whiled away the time cleaning the beast until it shined.

At lunchtime they all gathered in the main shack for their usual peaceful commune.

'Bastard!' yelled Slim, 'you can't be serious?'

'Too right I'm serious!' screamed Dave, 'If Uri can pay a thousand bucks a week to work here you should be able to cough up with at least a hundred.'

Slim stared him in the eye, 'Bullshit! You're just lucky I stay here 'cos if everyone knew what I know there'd be so many authorities on your back...', Slim ended the somewhat hollow threat lamely.

Dave paused, Slim was right, he knew most of the operation. He knew about the boxes, the night shift sludge and all the secrets of the mechanical worm. Damn, he's got a point.

Dave looked up. 'Alright then, we'll leave it as it is but I'm going down to the dole office and see if I can't get a New Start allowance or something for ya.'

Slim raised his eyes to the sky. ' I've worked here for over ten years you stupid twit so you ain't gonna get no New Start allowance.'

Dave was undeterred and jumped in the ute and headed to town.

Uri patiently observed all this and recognising a unique opportunity moved in.

'I'm sorry, Slim,' said Uri.

Slim looked at him. 'What?'

'I'm sorry,' repeated Uri. 'I have caused you trouble with Dave and I did not wish to do that.'

Slim shook his head, 'Nah mate, it's not you, it's that silly bastard,' pointing to the now dispersing trail of dust from Dave's ute. Slim shrugged his shoulders, 'Don't know why I put up with it,' he said and returned to his seat in the shack.

Uri leaned forward, 'Surely he is not that bad?' he asked.

Slim leaned back, 'Oh he can be a real bastard, mate. Some of the things he's made me do, well they weren't pleasant I can tell you.'

Uri, becoming more interested, leaned forward, 'Like what, Slim, what sort of things has he made you do?'

Slim may have been a slow country boy but that didn't mean he was stupid and he knew that talking about leading a protest on the bay would not be a wise thing to mention to a complete stranger. 'Oh lots of weird things. Like when we set up the worm farm out there in the middle of the dump,' said Slim.

Uri looked in the direction he had pointed. 'What worm farm, Slim? I don't see anything that looks like a worm farm.'

Slim pointed to the old water tank. 'See that tank? That's all that's left. Poor bastards just rolled over and died. Didn't stand a chance.'

Uri abandoned the topic as it seemed to lead nowhere. 'Slim,' he said, 'Dave said he did a study tour himself. Do you know what he looked at?'

Slim paused and gathered his thoughts, 'I wouldn't raise that topic with Dave if I was you. You see he went to France and whilst over there he met some bloke called Henri and this Henri bloke stitched him up good and proper. Dave has never forgiven him for that and it is a very sore point. If you have to mention it to him make sure that there's nothing nearby that he could hit you with.' Slim rubbed the top of his head, and remembered the last time he'd mentioned that trip to France.

Uri persisted, 'So did he buy anything from Henri?' he asked.

Slim was getting more cautious by the minute. 'No, mate, no money ever changed hands,' he said. 'Perhaps if you want some more info you'd better ask Dave?' and with that Slim turned and left the shack.

Uri realised that he had pushed too far, however he had learned some things from the discussion. Obviously Dave had not bought anything from Henri, therefore was he a supplier? But what could he have here that would be of interest to a commodity trader like Henri? It just didn't make sense. No this wasn't the answer that he had come to get. He was going to have to wait a bit longer and try again, perhaps with Dave himself this time. In the meantime there was nothing else to do so he moved out of the shack and off to the machinery shed to continue cleaning and servicing the machines.

* * *

It was a few hours later that Dave returned from his unsuccessful negotiation with the Australian Government and he was not in a happy mood. This much was obvious from the way his vehicle entered the site, basically sideways through the main gate, scattering people and animals. He then flipped it the other way and slid up to the shack, coming to a bone jarring halt against the concrete guttering and causing the remaining hubcap to pop off and roll away. He got out and slammed the door, all the time cursing the 'tight arsed, mean, mongrel, bastard government'. Dave headed into the shack and a rather unsuspecting Uri wandered over from the shed to chat with him.

Dave was still angry about the outcome of the meeting. This was obvious as parts and tools were being thrown to each corner of the shed. Uri had to duck as a screwdriver punctured the tin wall of the shed and exited near his head. Perhaps this was not the best time to talk to Dave but then again he couldn't think of any time that Dave was going to be approachable.

'Dave, can I have a word with you?' asked Uri. Dave looked up he was about to pass a word onto Uri when he paused and considered that if he upset this guy then a thousand bucks a week could go out the door, so a moderately polite Dave grunted, 'What?'

'When you were in France, Dave' continued Uri unaware of the likely repercussions of his act, 'did you meet a person by the name of Henri?'

'HENRI !' screamed Dave, 'HENRI! You mean that good for nothing, lying low life mongrel of a frog that runs the Paris tip?'

Uri taken aback at the vehemence of the response paused. 'Ah, yes, that is the Henri that I meant.'

'Well he's a mean, lying, cheating, mongrel bast... er, how do you know him, Uri?' asked Dave.

Uri smiled. 'Oh I know a lot about him, Dave. He is not a very honourable man. So tell me Dave, did you do a deal with him?'

Dave snorted, 'Yeah, we had a deal. I was going to take some of his rubbish for him but the bastard wouldn't pay. I put in a heap of work and incurred setting up costs for nothing. Christ if I had some way of getting back at that prick...'

'Well,' said Uri, 'perhaps I have something that you might be interested in. But I want you to answer a couple of questions for me first.'

Dave squirmed. 'What sort of questions?'

'Well, Dave, what sort of rubbish were you going to get rid of for Henri?' asked Uri.

Dave was rapidly loosing colour from his face now. 'I met up with the bastard on a study tour of foreign tips and he asked if I could dispose of some boxes for him. Now I came back here and made a hole in accordance with all the EPA regs and then he doesn't deliver!' He shrugged, 'So here I am, having spent a heap of money on consultants, EPA and everyone and I got nothing from it and that's why I'd like a chance to get even with that prick.'

Uri listened to the tale. Somehow it just didn't ring true but it was obvious that Henri had double-crossed Dave over some deal. Maybe Uri had been double-crossed too and there was nothing here to find. Yes maybe it was time to pay Henri back.

'Dave,' Uri began, 'did you know that Henri was a deserter from the French Foreign Legion?'

'You mean that bastard is a refugee from the army?' asked Dave incredulously.

'Yes', said Uri, 'apparently he abandoned his friends when they were in deep trouble and they have been looking for him ever since.'

Dave's face lit up. 'Uri, my old son,' he said, 'you don't happen to have a phone number for them do you?'

Uri jotted some figures down on a piece of paper and handed them to Dave. 'Certainly Dave, here you are,' he said.

Dave's face was split with an ear-to-ear grin as he took the number. 'Thanks Uri, you don't know how much I appreciate this.' Dave reached for his mobile phone and headed out into the dump so that he could make a private call.

Uri watched as he walked away. 'Yes, Dave, I think I shall stay here until I find out your secret, either from you or from Achmed and Yousef when they arrive,' he said quietly to himself and then he headed back into the dump to prepare for the onslaught that he felt was sure to come.

chapter 16

RUBBISH!

ACHMED AND YOUSEF PULLED INTO THE SECOND motel in town. All experienced terrorists knew that the first motel was going to be the most popular and thus if they were to remain in hiding they needed to be somewhere more secluded and less populated.

A hotel manager needs to be a soul of great discretion and tolerance. It is a difficult profession where almost all of your clients are called Smith and most want to haggle for an hourly rate on the room, and many for less than even that short period of time. Yes, things had greatly changed in the industry with the increase of Bed and Breakfast establishments. These little home industries had proven much more popular with the upper end of the market as there was only a few guests and thus much less chance of finding your partner, and theirs, occupying the room next door. Indeed the motel industry had taken a serious downturn in recent times. Now it seemed as if it was necessary to deal in sleaze or children's entertainment just to make ends meet, and Keith, the manager of the hotel, had never been fond of kids. However, even Keith was struggling to come to grips with the sight of the two that had pulled up outside.

They looked like something that had been formed by a cross between the films 'Lawrence of Arabia' and 'Scootermania'. A weird combination of flowing robes on brightly coloured scooters, one with a sidecar piled high with suitcases. The two were obviously of Arabic descent, but what would they be doing here. Oh well, shrugged Keith, a guest is a guest, and a guest is money.

Yousef and Achmed dismounted from their scooters and entered the foyer of the motel.

'Good evening, gentlemen,' said Keith dropping into his tired routine, 'can I help you?'

Achmed moved up to the counter, 'Yes,' he said, 'we would like a room'.

Keith looked at his booking sheet, which was empty, 'Hmm, I think we can fit you in. What name, Sir?'

'Smith,' answered Achmed.

Keith looked at the two of them, his eyebrows lifting only slightly. 'Yes, Mr Smith, one room with a queen size bed, is it?'

Achmed recoiled in shock 'No, No, we need two single beds.'

It was Keith's turn to be shocked, could this actually be a legitimate customer? 'Certainly, Mr Smith, and how long are you planning to stay?'

Achmed and Yousef looked at each other 'We are not sure, it may be a few days but it could be up to a week.'

Keith's face lit up, here was a long term customer for a change. 'Yes sir, Mr Smith, I will set you up in our finest room, the Presidential Suite.'

Achmed leaned forward and glanced down at the nameplate on the desk. 'Keith,' he said 'we are very private people and in our line of work we are very well known in our homelands and so whilst we are here we do not wish to be disturbed by anyone. Is that clear?'

Keith's mind was racing at the thought of who these people were. Finally he jumped to what he considered the most obvious conclusion that made sense; the funny dress, the scooters, the need for privacy.

'Oh I get it, you guys are rock and roll stars!' he said.

Achmed was shocked and was about to reach for a pistol to end any likely association between him and such an atheistic western-spawned abomination, but Yousef stepped in.

'Keith,' he started, 'we cannot let this get out because if it did then we would be mobbed by fans and we would have to leave immediately.'

That was the last thing that Keith wanted to happen. 'No, No,' he said quickly, 'your secret is safe with me.'

Yousef leaned on the counter and grabbed Keith's attention. 'Keith,' he said sliding a twenty-dollar note across the counter, 'can you tell me how we find a place called 'Dave's Dump.'

Keith was keen to help out a long-term customer and especially if it was one that knew how to tip. 'Sure', he replied, 'you go to the roundabout in the centre of town and take a left. It's about three kilometres outside of town. You can't miss it.'

Yousef smiled and slid another twenty-dollar note across the counter. 'Now', he smiled, 'can you tell us about Dave, what he looks like, how many work with him and all those details.'

Keith, anxious to help out someone who was obviously thinking of investing in Dave's new process spent the next hour detailing everything there was to know about Dave, his dump, and the business he conducted. Eventually it was a much more prepared pair that finally retired to the 'Presidential Suite'.

Achmed opened the door and they both entered cautiously. Somehow the suite did not quite meet their expectations of something that would be provided to a president. In many respects it simply appeared to be a normal hotel room, the beds, small table, two chairs, radio, TV and a small but functional bathroom. They shrugged, if this is how they treat their presidents then it is no wonder that they spend so much time in other countries.

Yousef dropped onto one of the beds, tired from the ride down. 'Achmed,' he said, 'tonight we rest but in the morning we will find this infidel and find the plutonium, then we can leave this forsaken place and take our rightful place in the heavens.' Achmed grunted agreement and the pair fell asleep dreaming of their moment of glory and the many celestial virgins that would await their tender care in the afterlife.

The morning sun greeted them and they felt much more refreshed from their deep sleep. A pleasant breakfast completed their preparations and then it was time to conduct the first reconnaissance of Dave's dump.

Yousef boarded his scooter and Achmed jumped into the sidecar. They followed Keith's directions and made their way out towards

Dave's Dump. The road was quite attractive and the bushland that lined each side of the road would provide good cover on the approach.

They continued down the road, riding past the dump. Their hearts raced as they saw it for the first time because they knew that here was their ticket to heaven and immortality. Yousef slowed and they both stared through the chain mesh fencing that surrounded the site, taking in the huts and machinery sheds. Achmed tried to pick out Dave but there were too many customers there.

Yousef pulled to the side of the road and turned to Achmed. 'What do you think?' he asked.

Achmed considered the question. 'It is a busy place this dump, perhaps we can enter and scout the area without being noticed.'

Yousef was not so sure but he decided not to argue so he turned their transport scooter around and headed for the dump. Fortunately for them Slim was on the gate that morning, not Uri, otherwise things may have gone very differently. Slim wandered up to the pair and asked, 'What have you got to dump, green waste, tyres, car bodies, scrap steel, concrete or general refuse?'

Yousef looked at him, 'We have nothing to dump, we just wish to have a look around.'

Slim was a bit taken aback by this. 'A look

around? This is a dump not an art gallery! If you're going to come here then you have got to have something to dump.'

Achmed dismounted from the sidecar. 'You cannot stop us, infidel. We want to look around your dump!' Yousef also dismounted and walked up to Slim, trying to further intimidate him.

This was a very bad move. Slim had played in the forward pocket enough to know every intimidation move that existed in the game of football and he had spent a lot of time with his brother in Sydney filling in for their ruby league team. Thus he grabbed Achmed by the shirt, pulled him close and looked him in the eyes, 'If you ain't got no rubbish then you're not coming in,' he snarled.

Dave had been watching this conflict from the comfort of the shed and he decided that it was time to step in, so he started towards the front gate.

Yousef spotted him first and just froze. Yes this was their man. The description matched perfectly. Achmed kept wriggling, trying to free himself from Slim until he too saw Dave approaching.

'Got a problem?' asked Dave.

Slim dropped Achmed. 'Nothing I can't handle,' he said.

'What's up?' pressed Dave.

Slim turned to him 'These guys turn up

wanting to look around the place but they haven't got any rubbish.'

Dave shook his head and grabbed them both by their collars, 'You can't come in here if you don't have any rubbish. That's what a dump is all about!' yelled Dave as he marched the pair back to their scooter. 'Now don't come back unless you have something to drop off,' Dave continued.

Dave turned and headed back towards the shed. Achmed and Yousef realising that they could do nothing quietly whilst there was such a crowd decided to board their scooter and retreat to consider their next action. They mounted and drove down the road about a kilometre and pulled off at a place where they could view the dump.

'That was him,' said Achmed.

'Yes,' agreed Yousef, 'that had to be Dave. The description from that low life, infidel dog, Keith, matched him perfectly.'

Achmed nodded. 'But how do we find the plutonium when there are too many people here during the day and how do we decide where to start?'

Yousef paused and thought about this for a few seconds. 'We need to conduct a series of visits and see if we can discover any basic infor-mation about the dump and then return under cover of night for some detailed exploration. But first we will need to get access to the dump and to do that we will need rubbish.'

'But where can we get rubbish from?' asked Achmed.

Yousef shrugged, 'Well, we will just have to adapt.' And so it was a strange pair that wandered into the business district that morning, moving from bin to bin collecting different materials to place into garbage bags bought from the local store. After a couple of hours they had gathered a few bags, which they brought back to their room. 'Now,' said Achmed, 'we will be able to visit the dump as many times as necessary.'

So this time they loaded up the sidecar with the bags of rubbish and Achmed rode on the seat behind Yousef. They retraced their route to the dump where Slim was still on the gate.

Slim smiled as they pulled up this time, 'Now you're getting the idea of this,' he said. 'So what type of rubbish do you have?'

Achmed looked at Yousef. 'What do you mean what type of rubbish do we have?' asked Yousef.

Slim shook his head. 'This is a recycling depot now not just a dump, you have to sort out the rubbish into the various types,' he said. Shaking his head he decided to take pity on these two. 'All right you two, take your bags of rubbish over there and sort it out to match the bins. Got it? Cans in the cans bin, steel in the steel bin, green waste in the green waste area, et cetera. Got it?' he asked.

Yousef and Achmed just nodded, glad to find a way past the front gate, and headed over to the area that Slim had indicated. Once there they unloaded their bags and surveyed the site. The hut was an obvious choice so they decided to discard that as a possible option. However the machinery shed was a more likely target as it was removed from the day-to-day operation. It seemed that there were only two people nearby, the ones called Slim and Dave, but it was impossible to tell how many were in the machinery shed. There were up to twenty others here dropping off rubbish into the various piles. There were too many members of the public milling around to do anything but look.

Achmed turned to Yousef, 'You start sorting the rubbish and I'll go and check things out.' So Yousef started emptying the bags and sorting out the rubbish with little enthusiasm whilst Achmed moved inconspicuously towards the shack.

He studied the layout of the shack, taking in the building itself, the two exits and the portaloo located at the back of the building. The vehicles were parked along one side against some concrete curb. The front gate included a shelter for a single person who was collecting the payments from the customers. He studied the machinery shed that was set further back. It was an open structure and he could make out a boat and some strange sort of machine that was open at the front. He thought he saw one person working on the large machine.

There were no obvious places where the plutonium would be stored except perhaps the machinery shed. He started out towards the shed.

'Oi!' came the call from the hut. Achmed froze and turned. Dave appeared in the doorway, 'Where do you think you're going?' he asked.

'I was going to have a look at your machine,' answered Achmed.

'Why?' asked Dave.

'I have heard so much about it and I would like to see it,' lied Achmed, looking around to see how many were watching. Unfortunately there were a few too many watching otherwise he would have shot this pig here and now.

'Are you on a government study tour?' asked Dave ever hopeful for an opportunity.

Achmed recoiled. 'N...no... I am here alone,' he stuttered.

Dave was irritated, here was a bloke who was obviously a foreigner and he wanted access to Dave's stuff without paying a cent. At least Uri was paying for what he was learning and then there was always the possibility of royalties to come. But this prick wanted to look round for free, well he had something else coming. Dave pierced him with his 'evil eye' stare. 'What do you want?'

Achmed had reached his limit. He did not take this treatment from anyone, especially a foreign unbelieving dog like Dave. He stared back, 'I want the material and you will not stop me from having it.'

Dave was not ready for this response. 'What material?' he said.

'Don't play with me, Dave,' snapped Achmed, 'I want the material,' he repeated.

Dave was at a loss. What was he talking about? Material? Was he some sort of feral dressmaker looking for a new fashion? Was it the mechanical worm? Did he want the plans for the worm? Perhaps he wanted some of the best stuff that Dave had hidden in various parts of the dump like the vintage Rolls Royce motor he'd buried in the far corner. That had to be it. This bloke must be some sort of international tip rat. He'd heard about people that roamed the globe looking for material that they could pick up for free and then sell at a large profit. Most usually roamed the swap meets but Dave had never come across one of them and certainly not in his dump. But there was no way this prick was going to get a lifetime of collecting for nothing.

Dave dug in ready for a fight. 'You'll get nothing from me you lousy tip rat!' said Dave.

Achmed had reached his limit now, and he leaned forward so that they were nose to nose. He decided that the best way to deal with this infidel would be to torture him slowly, no matter how many people were around, and with his mind made up he reached for the knife that was concealed beneath his clothes.

'Need some help, Dave?' asked Uri who had moved into position behind Achmed.

Achmed froze. One on one he was fairly confident that he could defeat Dave, but two against one? No, the odds were too great. He stared at Dave, 'We will continue this later,' and turned towards where the scooter was parked. Dave was unable to resist and he planted a size ten steel cap boot fair up his clacker.

Achmed spun around, 'You will pay for that you infidel dog!' He looked at Uri. 'You too will pay for what you have done here.' Uri just smiled and watched as Achmed returned to Yousef and they prepared to leave.

'A friend of yours?' asked Uri.

'Nah,' said Dave, 'just some stuck up mongrel trying to steal my ideas and my stuff.'

Uri looked at him. 'I think you have made a strong enemy there, Dave, and I would not take his threat lightly.'

Dave snorted, 'I have had many more threaten me with worse than that on virtually every Saturday night for the last twenty years.'

He paused. Come to think of it he had faced far worse with Caroline's father, and even his own mother.

Uri was not so convinced. 'Dave,' he said, 'if you don't mind I would like to prepare a few surprises for our Arab friends just in case they come back.'

Dave shrugged and started to walk away calling over his shoulder 'Yeah, whatever, I don't think they have the guts but perhaps we should make sure.'

Uri smiled to himself and watched until the scooter pulled out of sight. He had recognised Achmed and Yousef and he had no doubt that they would keep coming back until they obtained whatever it was that they were searching for and when they did he would be here waiting. Uri had most of his surprises ready but now with Dave's permission he could activate them, and so he busied himself for the rest of the day putting things into place.

* * *

They arrived back at the motel with more than just their pride dented. Achmed's ride back had not been pleasant due to the bruising around his ring. Dave did not know it but he had made a very formidable enemy, one who would not rest until he had crushed Dave into the ground and scattered his pieces to the four winds. No one treated Achmed like that and lived, and it was a trend that he was going to ensure continued. He would not rest now until his revenge was complete.

They staggered back to their hotel room, angry at the results of the frontal assault they had just attempted. Achmed thrust the door open and screamed, 'That infidel Dave must die! It is a personal Jihad between him and me now and by the beard of the prophet it shall be he who dies!'

Yousef waited patiently whilst this tirade continued and when it ebbed he leaned over. 'I assume then, Achmed, that you did not locate the plutonium?'

Achmed glared at him, 'No I did not, but I will not rest until both it and vengeance is mine.'

'Night is for the hunter,' continued Achmed, 'and I will hunt. Tonight it would be best to work alone like the leopard in the jungle,' he concluded and so he determined that he'd get better results unhindered by infidels that wished to foil his plans. He would also do better without Yousef to distract him, he decided.

He turned to Yousef. 'Stay here and entertain yourself. I will go back to the dump and get the material and deal with that dog, Dave, if Allah is willing.'

It was a cool night when he left the hotel and he decided to jog to Dave's dump. He was fit, having honed his muscles and body in the training camps of Libya many times, and he prized himself on being able to run far from his enemies when required. He set a reasonable pace as he lightly jogged towards his objective, ignoring the cars that passed him, their drivers bemused by a jogger with a checked tea-towel on his head.

When Achmed arrived at the gate to the complex he assumed there would be no guard on the gate and that he'd have time to search at his leisure. For all intents and purposes that seemed to be the case. However, Uri had decided that a strategic guard on the dump was required, aware that the Arabs were likely to attempt to infiltrate the area soon. He had no fear that he would be out-smarted by them, although being out-gunned was a real possibility. So he'd spent considerable time over the previous nights setting up a series of innovative booby-traps that would foil terrorists, as well as deranged teenage lovers that wished to get amorous in a smelly environment. As much as the latter seemed ridiculous, he had found enough used prophylactics lately to convince him that there were such lunatics in the area. When he began to muse as to it perhaps being Dave he had stopped the thought immediately as the visual image in his mind made him shudder.

Uri was confident enough of his traps to take a position away from the dump, sitting camouflaged on a neighbouring hill of garden mulch that overlooked the area. Night vision binoculars assisted him. The sound of someone climbing the gate, negotiating the barbed wire at the top, failing to completely clear it, and screaming in a muffled but painful way as he lightly scraped his scrotum, alerted Uri to the arrival of his quarry.

Achmed walked slowly, now with a slight limp, around the initial section of the dump and made for the rear. This was the as yet unexplored region that he felt was the most obvious place to hide nuclear material. There was a small trench in the way that had a very smelly and somewhat fetid gunge flowing like a mixture of treacle, vomit and two-day-old flat beer, along its length. A small makeshift wooden bridge crossed it, approximately three planks wide and 6 feet long. Achmed approached the bridge and stepped on to it, his thoughts set in the future as he determined his search pattern. As his foot placed some weight onto the wooden bridge, a superbly manufactured booby-trap, looking like a spring-loaded, up-ended frying pan was activated. It slammed a patch of eight-inch nails right through the flimsy wooden boards and perfectly impaled Achmed's right foot.

'Aaagh!' Achmed screamed, instinctively

175

pulling his foot up to hop around in pain, except that his foot was nailed to the plank now and the attempt to raise that leg resulted in him falling head first, forward onto the bridge. The full weight of his fall allowed the second stage of the trap to work, collapsing the bridge in the middle and plunging Achmed into the flow of muck in the trench. His face submerged for two seconds, then bobbed up again and the full stench of the material entered his flared nostrils, burning them like salt on an open wound. A second scream emanated from Achmed's mouth, allowing a drip of the trench fluid to be tasted.

From Uri's position the entire episode was hilarious and the attempt to stay quiet made his night vision binoculars bob around as his chest heaved with mirth. He watched as his enemy, with considerable difficulty pulled his foot out of the board, then hopped around, back on dry land after scrambling up from the trench. He grabbed a piece of the broken board and smashed it repeatedly against the ground, screaming abuse in what Uri assumed to be less than polite Arabic. This lasted for quite a while. Ten minutes later, limping profoundly now, Achmed hobbled forward to a hill of old metallic objects and began to fling them around. Pots and pans and bits of electrical apparatus flew everywhere. A washing machine shell rumbled down the pile and steel sheeting slid away to reveal more rusty objects.

Achmed seemed to become discouraged after twenty minutes of fruitless activity and wandered, still lopsidedly, towards a pile of paint tins.

Oh, good, thought Uri, smiling once more.

Achmed kicked the pile of tins, some eight cans high and twenty deep. There was a shudder and Achmed's eyes registered that he had committed another error, as an old one-litre paint tin of oil based Wattyl Solarguard almost took his head off as it flew with phenomenal speed directly at his head.

Amazing what 2 grams of plastic explosive and a trembler switch can do, Uri thought.

Achmed watched in disbelief as the paint can grazed the top of his head by a whisker, due to his instinctive ducking motion, and sliced a faint groove along his hairline. If he had retained his kefia, rather than allowed it to float away in the trench, it would have saved him completely. The can had also expelled its contents as it flew westward, so Achmed now looked as if he was supporting the regime of Saudi Arabia, its flag's vivid green colouring neatly dripping down his shoulders, arms and face. He stood there, motionless now, too angry as well as frightened, to speak or scream. Allah was mocking him. How else could the elements transpire to humiliate him in this fashion?

He did not wish to be defeated by whatever unknown force was spoiling his plans. He did not know whether Dave had arranged somehow for these mishaps to occur or if luck was against him. Everything was written, as the Koran told him, so for some reason tonight was obviously not the right night to advance his aims. It was a sign from Allah. Time to retire and take out his frustration on Yousef. He hobbled back towards the gate, then stood looking up at the barbed wire that had partially tattooed his scrotum, a now minor issue in the list of events of the evening. Words failed him as he began a weary climb up the gate, being extremely careful as he negotiated his exit and walked slowly and painfully back towards the hotel.

Uri watched him leave, chuckling out loud when he was able to do so without being heard. Then he wandered back to the dump's main area and reset a few traps and checked the priming mechanisms on others. It had been a very profitable night.

When Achmed arrived back at the hotel he found Yousef 'relaxing' while watching a German soft-porn film on SBS television. Achmed entered the room as Yousef exited elements of himself over the cover of a Woman's Day magazine. Yousef had his hands full, or one of them at least, as Achmed came up to him. The blow from Achmed knocked Yousef off the bed and out cold. There were no words left.

Achmed looked to the ceiling, 'Allah, what do I do? Give me a sign. Should I kill Yousef for you for his selfish action, or use him in other ways?' He sat heavily on the bed and waited for Yousef to wake up. To accelerate the process he urinated on him. It was the least he could do even if it did make his scrotum hurt, he decided. Yousef must suffer, as he had done.

When Yousef regained consciousness, Achmed made him serve him. Yousef washed Achmed in the bath, scrubbing and scraping the paint off him, then, after drying him he administered to Achmed's foot wound and performed relaxation acts upon him to make up for the different ways in which the two men had spent their evening.

At the conclusion of these Yousef stared at the ceiling and decided that he will always insist on going to the dump with Achmed from now on no matter what dangers were there as it had to be better than the consequences of staying at home entertaining himself.

chapter 17

ACHMED AWOKE SLOWLY THE NEXT MORNING,
but his hatred for Dave had continued to build
overnight and as he reached consciousness he
realised that most of the obscene acts he had
planned for Dave had actually been perpetrated on his pillow. This had left the pillow a little
flat and Achmed a little embarrassed. Yousef
had awoken early after little sleep and had observed most of this and was just glad that it
hadn't been him.

'Achmed,' Yousef began, 'I think that you

183

should stay here today and I will try and find the plutonium.'

Achmed sneered, 'Fool! What makes you think that you will do any better there than I did?'

Grinning, Yousef said, 'Well Achmed, you have assumed that he would hide it at the dump, correct?' Achmed nodded. Yousef continued, 'Well it is possible that instead he has hidden it at his home and that the dump is simply a ploy to confuse people like ourselves.'

'That is possible,' agreed Achmed, still unsure that Dave was smart enough to think of such a strategy. 'It is worth investigating more.'

Yousef smiled, 'And that is exactly what I shall do today whilst you remain here and recover.'

Achmed also smiled because he guessed that if Dave had protected his dump so well then it was safe to assume that his home security would be even more impressive. But if this fool wanted to try then so be it, and let Allah decide his fate.

Yousef, content with his idea, trotted out to see Keith who was relaxing at the front desk. One of the perks of running a motel where everyone only stays an hour or less is that there is usually no one around demanding breakfast and so he had grown used to the idea of sleeping late each day. He yawned and put down the paper as Yousef approached.

'Hi, Yousef,' he called, 'what can I do for you today? Bacon and eggs? Some more of those Rabbi approved pork schnitzels that I get from the supermarket?'

Yousef considered for a moment, 'Hmm, send in both, for my colleague is in need of tender care this morning.'

'Oh,' replied Keith, 'a big night out eh? Hit the turps a bit did he?'

Yousef paused wondering how much did Keith know. 'No, it appears that the turps hit him. Anyway, that is not why I am here. Keith, tell me, where does Dave live?'

Keith didn't understand the significance of the question but never one to upset a long term client he continued on, 'Sure I know, it's just outside of town. You head towards the dump, go about a K out of town, turn left and go for about two K's down the dirt road. It's a huge mansion on your right on top of the hill. You can't miss it.'

Yousef jotted himself a few notes, thanked Keith and headed out to where his scooter was parked. Cautious after what had happened to Achmed he decided that he had better take some weapons with him in case the house was also well defended. Then, with the scooter appropriately loaded he boarded and headed out towards Dave's place.

It was a pleasant country drive, not that Yousef noticed the scenery as he was far more concerned with his plans of what to do when he got there. As he reached the turn off for Dave's place a battered old ute came straight out in front of him, sliding sideways it swerved violently towards the dump. So sharp did it turn that the dog chained to the back was held perfectly horizontal with the road for what seemed ages until the chain, gravity, and bad driving brought him crashing back to the deck of the ute where he promptly turned, barking and snapping at the driver.

It had only been a momentary encounter but Yousef had recognised the figure driving. It had definitely been Dave and this presented him with a wonderful opportunity, as now he knew the place should be empty. With increased confidence he continued on towards Dave's place.

The road was rough and the scooter bounced around a lot but Yousef managed through good luck and some skills to keep it heading down the track. He splashed through the puddle at the bottom and began the climb up to the top of the hill. As he cleared the trees, there it was, situated right on top of the hill just as Keith had said. Indeed it was a mansion, with sweeping lawns and a columned front.

Yousef pulled up at the entrance to the drive-way and contemplated his next move. It seemed like the place was empty. Obviously Dave was gone but there could be someone else there, he thought. There were no cars visible and no sign of anyone in the garden, not that he could see round the back. But, just to be sure, it seemed sensible to leave the scooter and make his way forward on foot.

Cautiously he made his way along the drive-way, darting from tree to tree, trying to remain unseen. As the trees came to an end he dropped to the ground and leopard crawled between the beds of petunias until he reached the stairs. He ducked down to the side of the stairs and then slowly made his way up. Reaching the door, he tried the handle but it was locked.

'Hmm,' mumbled Yousef, 'I will have to try around the back. It is just too visible here to try breaking in.' With equal care he moved along the side of the building to the back yard that had been hidden from his view.

As the reached the corner he very carefully extended his neck until he could view the yard, which was when he saw her. Not a complete view, just the bottom half, as the rest was hidden by the towels that she had pegged out on this side of the rotary washing line. The big rear end reminded him of Nefertiti. She had been one of his first romances during his time at University in Dubai. Those had been simpler times when you could make love for the joy of doing so. Later he came to learn the dangers of this pastime when all your colleagues are terrorists. There are many factions amongst terrorist organisations, much as there are in any political party, and the rivalry between them can be immense. It had been noted that on some occasions female members had conducted a suicide mission against a terrorist of the other faction using a strategically located device with a simple push button used to activate it. This was placed deep enough that it would only come into use on the 'pepper' stroke. You could say that they came together before they were blown apart. Safe sex it wasn't, and a condom would never protect you from this practice. Remembering the ordeal of last night, Yousef took some pleasure in the fact that nature had given Achmed a natural defence against such an attack.

But Nefertiti had just enjoyed life and they had revelled in the fun of it all. 'Hmm,' whispered Yousef, 'maybe I should review my commitment to this suicide mission. I had forgotten that there is a lot to live for.' He looked wistfully at the figure in front of him. Unfortunately it was then that she spun the clothesline round to peg out the next row, exposing herself to Yousef's full view.

Yousef choked and made a strange spluttering

sound and tried to withdraw himself from sight before she saw him.

Dave's Mum looked away defensively, but had noticed the tea towel on his head. 'Mmm,' she considered, 'either he is mental patient with a strange bandage or perhaps, just perhaps, he is one of those boat people.'

It didn't seem to worry her that she was located at least 100 kilometres from the coast and that the chance of a boat from the Middle East arriving on the south east coast was about a million to one. Indeed the only likely source of such a boat would be either Tasmania or New Zealand and for some reason the Government had stopped trying to prevent people from either place from getting in.

She looked around. There was Dave's shack nearby but that didn't offer anything. Come to think of it, if he was a burglar then he was welcome to help himself to whatever he could find there with her blessing. That should teach Dave a lesson for leaving her alone with mongrels like this prowling around. No, the house seemed like the best place to head and so she moved slowly towards the door, acting as if she had never seen him. She quickly stepped inside and slammed the door shut and activated the dead locks. But what to do now?

'Should I call the police?' she wondered, but somehow that seemed futile. The last time she had called was when she had asked them to re-move Dave because he was loitering. They had been polite but they kept insisting that it was his property and that he was therefore allowed to loiter anywhere he liked. 'Nah', she said, 'those buggers wouldn't do anything anyway, most of 'em are a bunch of bleeding hearts and they'll probably tell me that I have to adopt the bastard or something.'

She headed upstairs so that she could get a bird's eye view of what the mongrel was up to. From the second floor she could see him sneaking around the back yard. He headed into Dave's shack and didn't reappear for about ten minutes. When he re-emerged he paused as if looking for something. When he couldn't find anything else that seemed to interest him in the yard he started towards the house.

Yousef had finished searching the shack out the back. He had found nothing of interest. Well that's not true. He found lots of things in the shack of interest to red-blooded males and one strange mud covered pig suit but he found no signs of plutonium anywhere. He assumed that this must be the gardener's shack as it wasn't really fit for human habitation. He viewed the mansion and decided that he would have to search there despite the woman he had seen.

'This is it,' Mum stated, 'well I'm not giving in to no bloody foreigner!' With that thought she ran to the bedroom and grabbed a 50-foot bull-whip. It had belonged to her fourth husband, a bullocky who used to traverse the Canning stock route. He'd been a good husband and he always said that sitting on the cart watching the bullocks sway in front of him had always reminded him of her. Something he'd proved every time they met.

Yes, he had been a good husband and outstanding with a whip. He had even taught her to use it and she could crack it with the best of them. Snapping a cigarette from someone's mouth at fifty feet was nothing. These days it usually took two goes to hit a fly in flight but a little practice would restore her aim.

She looked down at the basket that lay at the base of the bed, and the bull terrier that rested there. 'C'mon, Cutie, we've got visitors,' she encouraged. Cutie grinned that sort of evil grin that only a bull terrier can, and rose from the basket with anticipation in his eyes.

Cutie was not a pretty dog but then again neither was his owner. Dave hated this dog with a passion and often added another letter to his name and Cutie took every opportunity to respond to Dave's kindness in a like fashion.

Yousef moved to the back door but it was locked. Still, no great problem, he thought. He headed over to the washing line and grabbed a towel, which he placed over the window. One sharp tap and it broke with only a muffled sound. He carefully removed the pieces, put his arm through the gap and undid the latch and then made his way into the house.

He stood up and looked around, absolutely dumbfounded. Never before had he seen such opulence. The floor was white marble with a sweeping staircase moving up the central part. Gold and crystal chandeliers hung from the ceiling and antique furniture decorated each corner of the room.

In awe, he moved from room to room, each seeming to be better than the last. He finally arrived at the bathroom.

It was amazing. He had seen pictures of what they thought the great Roman baths looked like, but this was magnificent. The columns soared to the ceiling, the bath was deep and luxurious, showers were located at the end and toilets were placed in the corner. A full-length mirror was fixed to the wall next to the bath. Yousef looked down at himself and remembered the 'work' he had done last night. To bathe in a room such as this became his immediate obsession.

'It would be good to rest here,' he said. 'I do not think that she saw me and so I can afford some time.' He closed the door, then reached down and turned on the hot water taps.

Mum, hearing the water starting to run, turned to Cutie, 'C'mon darling we know where he is now,' and slowly they made their way down the stairs.

Yousef waited until the bath filled, added some scented oil from a nearby bottle and then stripped and entered the hot water. The water caressed his body, leaving him feeling clean as he relaxed, surrounded by the crispness of the marble and the gold plated taps. He could feel the weight of the world lifting from his shoulders.

'Still,' he said softly, 'I cannot remain here too long,' and so after ten minutes he begrudgingly lifted himself from the bath. He moved to the far end of the room where the towels hung opposite the full-length mirror. Glimpsing sideways, he looked at his reflection. His strong, lean body cut a fine figure. He couldn't help himself and he turned sideways and struck the classic bodybuilder pose with both arms lifted up level with his shoulders. He grinned and then doubled over as his groin exploded two seconds after the bathroom door crashed open.

Now it is probably not fair to compare his penis to a cigarette, as a cigarette was slightly smaller but to a trained bullocky it was an easy target and she expertly made contact tip to tip.

'Go, Cutie!' she yelled, and the dog rushed forward to Yousef and sank his teeth deep into the exposed left buttock.

Finding his breath, Yousef screamed in pain and tried to make for the exit but it was difficult with the pain and a mad dog attached to his rear. He shuffled as fast as he could out of the bathroom and back into the hall. He was further encouraged when the whip cracked again, clipping his right cheek.

'Cutie, here!' yelled Mum, and the dog let go. Yousef seized the opportunity and leapt on the dog sinking his own teeth into its throat as he had been taught in Afghanistan. It was an amazing show of strength as can only be attributed to a desperate man as he picked the dog up in his teeth and shook it like a cat would shake a rat. Cutie struggled but it was in vain and slowly his eyes glazed and he went limp. Yousef, no longer feeling any resistance, let go of the lifeless body, spat out a mouthful of dog hair and stood staring at Mum.

For a moment he considered doing the same to this devil as she stood frozen with horror from watching Cutie's demise. He took one step forward, which jerked her into action and she raised the bullwhip high, ready to strike. Yousef's groin still ached from the first blow and so he decided that retreat would be better. He turned and ran with all his might, through the house and to the window through which he had entered. He dived through and, suddenly acutely conscious of his nakedness he grabbed a few items from the washing line as he ran past and headed down the driveway.

Naked, bleeding, and with a great throbbing in his groin he slumped over the fence post at the end of the driveway. He also had failed. This 'She Devil' had destroyed him. But what could he do? He could not admit that a mere old woman had defeated him! So he turned and slowly made his way down to where he had left the scooter. Once he reached it he instinctively reached for the trouser pocket where he had left the keys only to realise that his clothes, keys, guns, and knives were all still inside the house with the Devil and the now dead wolf. He looked at the items he had grabbed in that mad rush past the line, a bra, a small T-shirt that must have belonged to a child and a mismatched pair of socks.

He struggled into the T-shirt, which fitted like a lycra crop top and then improvised a pair of jocks using the bra as a cup and tying the socks together as a belt. The double D cup left him with more than enough room, even allowing for the swelling.

Longingly he looked at the scooter. This would have been ideal but the keys were still in the house. Yousef contemplated returning and getting them but it was likely that she had already called the police and so he resigned himself to a long walk back, pushing the scooter beside him.

Hours later he knocked on the door of the motel room, which Achmed answered. He stared at Yousef as he pushed his way into the room.

Yousef spun and said 'Do not ask, just know that the time for vengeance is now!'

chapter 18

DAVE WAS RELAXING BACK AT THE DUMP BUT his mind wasn't on the job any more. 'It's no good. I have to see her,' Dave said quietly. He'd been thinking again of Caroline and the games they liked to play. This was partly inspired by the books Slim had left scattered around the office. There was no question that she was the best woman he'd ever been with, and he admitted to himself that she was probably the only one he'd ever be happy to see on a regular basis, like every day in the same bed. That was a huge admission for Dave, whose main turn on was money, coupled with his preferred means of getting it, like running the biggest dump in the Southern Hemisphere. But Caroline was increasingly on his mind, especially during the week following the time that she'd been on other parts of his anatomy. He had experienced many near death experiences lately and now he wanted some serious life experiences to compensate. In short he wanted her again. It was more than a physical need. She understood him, without the requirement for words. They would look into each other's eyes, accept the fact that neither of them was attractive to the majority of the population, and revel in the joy of mutual understanding and physical desire. Yes, Caroline was the girl for him.

But the danger! Her old man would kill him if given the slightest chance. But some desires are so strong that even death is an acceptable risk.

He needed a detour from his pick-up route, via the pig farm. But would her old man be there? He'd have to get rid of the old bastard. It was worth a phone call anyway. He picked up the phone and dialled her number, scraping off bits of muck from the handset as he waited impatiently for the ringing to be answered by her gruff voice.

'Yep?' she answered.

Thank God, Dave thought. 'It's me, Caroline, Dave,' he began.

She mellowed immediately. 'Well, well, what a nice surprise. What's up, Dave?' she asked.

'Is your old man around the farm today?' Dave began, 'Because if not I thought I'd pop over and see you, if you wanted me to that is?'

'I'll get rid of him. When will you be here?' she said.

'Twenty minutes?' Dave suggested, his trousers starting to bulge with the anticipation of their meeting.

'No problem,' she replied. 'And Dave?'

'Yes?'

'Forget the pig suit. There's no time for that. Just come in the back door and upstairs,' she panted.

Dave dropped the phone on the cradle and hurried out of the office. Slim was looking at him as he passed by on the way to his new truck. Dave shouted, 'I'm off to do a valuation, back in a few hours!'

Slim wasn't sure how you place a value on a bag of rubbish but he had learnt not to question Dave's strange comings and goings. He just shrugged 'Okay; you going to come back before knock off?'

'Yeah I should be here to help wind things up,' called Dave as he jumped into the truck and headed off.

As he approached the pig farm his trouser pouch started to bulge again, and he squirmed a little in anticipation of Caroline's form. She appeared at the front door before he'd even stopped the truck. His eyes went wide, in a similar way to a sheep's when it gets a surprise from an unexpected affection. She was wearing an apron, and nothing else, her ample breasts poking, or rather, flowing out of the sides. He almost ran from the truck and as he did so she also ran, away and to the side of the house and towards the barn at the rear. She was quite fast for such a large girl and the sight of her proportions wobbling in the way that endeared her to him made Dave run faster. She made it to the barn just ahead of him and flopped down on some hay bales that had been prepared with a checked blanket. There were a couple of bottles of beer nearby as well.

As Dave caught up to her and descended to her prone form, she opened her legs and pinned him like an expert wrestler. He was trapped, but in a place he was happy to be. She grabbed the beer bottles with her meaty right arm and with her left twisted off the tops.

'Have a beer, Dave,' she laughed as she tightened her grip.

He couldn't help but laugh with her, through the slight pain of his amorous incarceration. 'Geez, you're a bonza sheila, Caroline. If you uncover a pizza next I'll marry you on the spot,' he chuckled.

'Stuff that, Dave. Do I look like I've got a flat head, you pervert,' she kidded. Get that beer down and get your strides off,' she ordered.

He didn't need any further prompting and finished the beer with one hand while extricating himself from his clothing with the other. He watched as she ripped the apron off and revealed herself to him.

The nearby pigs could only hear the unusual yet slightly familiar sounds of coupling as they munched away on their recent slops. The squeals were somehow comforting to the many piglets that were nuzzling their sows for milk. At the end of the half-hour of sweaty love-making Dave gave a massive groan of delight, matching Caroline's own noises and they flopped down on the ground, exhausted and satiated.

'Dave,' Caroline gasped, 'you know we're made for each other don't you?' she stated simply.

'I do, Caroline, I do,' he agreed without a hint of fear at this sudden commitment to their unusual relationship.

'Dave, I know it's not a good question to ask, but, have you slept with other women?' asked Caroline a concerned look on her face.

Dave froze. He knew that this was the make or break question and he knew that anything less than complete honesty would leave him in trouble in the future. He looked deep into her eyes and said 'No, I can't say that I've ever slept with any.' Which was true, sure they had sex but he'd never slept with them.

'So, what are we going to do about it then?' she asked, without any pressure in her question.

'Buggered if I know at this stage. There's the little problem of your father's hatred for me, isn't there?' Dave asked her.

'Not hatred, Dave, just contempt. He just wants to make sure that his little girl is going to be looked after, that's all,' she said.

'Funny way of showing it if you ask me. Shotguns don't leave much room for conversation,' Dave snorted.

'Well, we'll just have to find a way to bring him round, love, that's all. Won't we?' she whispered.

Dave kept quiet. He was sure that the only way he wanted to bring her mad bastard of a father round was with the assistance of a front-end loader. There was a nice little spot in his dump for the prick. A burial fit for the man's character, built over an old septic tank. The image of it all made Dave smile, which Caroline took to be bliss at their recent activities and unspoken engagement. Dave rolled on his side and she snuggled in closer. Dave smiled and leaned back, staring at the barn roof. But how, he wondered.

Boing!

Dave turned his eyes to see what had caused that noise only to see the prongs of a still vibrating pitchfork straddling his member. He looked round to see his worst nightmare standing at the entrance to the barn.

'You bastard! You've defiled my daughter and now you're going to pay!' yelled Caroline's Dad.

Dave extracted himself carefully from between the prongs and stood up using the apron still lying beside him to cover what he could. Not that he was modest just that it's harder to hit a hidden target. Caroline also jumped up and grabbed the blanket.

'I'm going to kill you with my bare hands!' Caroline's father raged and leapt towards Dave.

Caroline roughly pushed Dave aside and placed herself in the path of her charging father. 'No, Dad!' she yelled back, 'you can't. I love him and we're going to get married!'

This stopped him in his tracks. Caroline and Dave married? Dave as a son in law? Babies? Grandchildren? But why Dave? Why not the nice man at the pig food store? Or the young fella at the slaughter yard? How about the man who pumped the septic tanks? Anyone else, but not Dave!

His confusion grew and it was obvious to all that he was suffering a great deal in trying to accept this news. It was a simple choice of whether he would resolve the issue in his head or have a stroke.

He finally reached a conclusion. 'I'll go and put an end to all this nonsense,' he said, as he turned and headed out to his car. Everyone knew that Dave was a pawn to his mother and that is where Caroline's father decided to go to try and stop this from happening. He plunged the key in the ignition, twisted it viciously, gunned the motor, slammed the car into gear and headed out onto the road.

Caroline and Dave looked at each other. 'Well,' said Dave, 'I guess I just had another near death experience and things can't get any worse can they?' He grabbed her and they both fell back on the hay bales again. 'One more time and then I better get back to the dump,' he said. Caroline just smiled.

* * *

Meanwhile Caroline's father continued driving wildly towards Dave's place. He had to see Dave's mother and put a stop to this ridiculous situation. There was no way that he could allow Dave to become his son-in-law; it wasn't fair to him or his daughter. He just didn't want that smelly bastard hanging around the house, mauling his daughter, sponging off him and his farm. He pushed the old Morris 10 to new limits, reaching a new high speed of ninety-five kilometres per hour, ignoring the protest from the side valve engine as the valve bounce and piston slap hammered together in an incredible crescendo of noise.

He drove the old Morris along the road to Dave's place as hard as he could. As he made the turn into the dirt road to Dave's house he swerved to avoid an obviously drug-crazed lunatic running along the road pushing a scooter and wearing nothing but a tight T-shirt and bra. And even then he hadn't got the latter items in the right bloody places. Society was definitely falling down around him. Well at least that loony wasn't shagging his daughter or worse still trying to marry her. His whole body shook with the repulsion of the idea of Dave becoming part of his family.

Wildly he slid the car into the driveway and headed up to the main entrance where he left the car parked on the third step. He exited and headed up to the front door and knocked hard only to have it swing open with the blow. Surprised he carefully put his head around the door to see why the security was so lax.

'Hello!' he called loudly, but there was no answer. He tried again but still there was no response. Cautiously he entered the hallway. Even he was taken aback with the beauty of this place. 'Perhaps there is a side to Dave I've never seen,' he thought. Quietly he pushed the next door open and then recoiled as the door jam next to him splintered apart as a shotgun blast ripped into it.

A hysterical female screamed out, 'You got Cutie, you bastard, but you're not going to get me!'

'Hey Lady, put that gun down,' he called back, 'I think you've got the wrong bloke. I'm here to talk to you about Dave.'

There was a few seconds pause and then the voice said, 'OK, come out where I can see you and just remember I ain't afraid to use this.'

He took a deep breath and went through the door. The sight that greeted him was heart wrenching. The old lady was kneeling on the floor cradling the body of a dog with one arm and the shotgun with the other. Blood had soaked her trousers and it was obvious that something had ripped the throat out of the dog. The glazed look in its eyes showed that it was dead. He wasn't sure about the lady; it was hard to tell if she had been injured or if all that blood was just from the dog. When she saw him she visibly relaxed, dropping the shotgun to the floor and then collapsing over the dog sobbing uncontrollably.

Something major had happened here, but

what? He moved towards her. 'What happened here? Are you hurt?' he asked in a soothing voice.

Slowly she brought the sobbing under control and looked up at him. She studied him intently and with growing interest. 'I think it was one of them boat people,' she said, 'the bastard broke in here, used the bathroom as if he owned the place and when I asked him to leave he attacked me and killed my dog. Just used his hands and his teeth to rip, sob,…. If Cutie hadn't been here….' With that, she again collapsed sobbing over the dog.

It was obvious that he was going to get nowhere until he could get her away from the dog's corpse. 'Come on,' he soothed, 'let me take care of your dog. Cutie was it?'

She sniffed and looked up at him still unsure whether to trust him 'What are you going to do with him?'

'He deserves a hero's burial and that's what I'll give him,' he said.

She looked deep into his eyes, 'You're a nice man. What's your name?'

He returned the gaze, 'Patrick,' he answered, 'and what's yours?'

'Gertrude. Funny I haven't heard that name since my last husband died. Usually for the last fifty years I've always been called Mum,' she replied.

'Well, Gertrude,' he said with a smile, 'why don't you give me Cutie and I'll take care of him while you get yourself cleaned up and changed.'

She hesitated but he was such a kind man, 'OK,' she answered, and she helped lift the dead dog's body into his arms.

Patrick picked the dog's body up and headed out the back door. But where was he to put it? He looked around. There seemed to be nowhere obvious. 'Hmm I'll check this gardener's shack and see if there's anything I can use.' He entered the shack. It was a mess, everything had been rummaged through and upended but there were no obvious tools anywhere. The only thing of real interest was a strange pig suit. Somehow it seemed familiar. Looking around further he spotted what was either a rough bed or more likely a dog's basket and this seemed as good as any other spot and so he placed the dead body into the bed and covered it with a blanket. He then returned to the house.

'Gertrude,' he called, 'are you alright?'

'I'm OK, come into the kitchen, I've made a pot of tea,' she answered, still a little dazed.

Patrick followed the sound of her voice and went into the kitchen. She had changed her clothes and washed the dog's blood from her hands and face. In fact now the crisis was over he noticed that she was quite an attractive woman, about his age too. Sure she was large, but large women had never repulsed him. And she was so polite as well.

'Milk?' she asked waking him from his study of her.

'Oh, er, yes please and one sugar.'

They both sat at the kitchen table and took comfort in the mundane ritual of tea. After a pause whilst both sipped their tea Gertrude asked, 'So why are you here? You're not another one of those retirement home salesmen sent by Dave are you?'

He recoiled. How could Dave treat his mother like this? 'No, I wanted to talk to you about Dave though. You see he wants to marry my daughter.'

It was Gertrude's turn to be shocked. Dave married? But then the good-for-nothing laya-bout would really want his home back and he would have justifiable grounds to get it. 'Who is it that he wants to marry?' she asked.

'It's my daughter, Caroline,' said Patrick, 'she's just an innocent child and doesn't know what she really wants. First it was a pony, then a pet pig and now she wants Dave. I'm sure it's only a passing thing but I don't want her get-ting hurt.'

'I know how you feel,' said Gertrude. 'I'm worried about Dave. I mean what if Cutie's murderer wasn't a boat person but some nutcase who was after Dave, not me, and I just happened to be here. Could you, and I know this is a big imposition, get a message to Dave and tell him to watch out for that man.'

Warning Dave of impending danger was the last thing on his mind but what else could he say. 'OK, I'll try. But what are we going to do about him and Caroline?'

Gertrude hesitated. 'I know it's selfish but I don't really want him marrying anyone, Patrick, not even your Caroline. I can see you feel the same way so perhaps we could work together for our mutual benefit?'

'That would be fine with me; thank you for your understanding,' said Patrick.

Gertrude decided to push her luck even further, 'Well how about letting me show you the extent of my gratitude for your help with both Dave and Cutie,' she said as she reached down and cupped him. Patrick stood stunned for a moment as the extent of the offer struck home but then he blurted, 'I'll just get something from the shed and be right back.' He rushed outside, grabbed the pig suit and returned. She looked at it and at him and smiled, remembering her third husband the sheep farmer with the velcro gloves. 'Should fit perfectly,' she said and then she took him by the hand and led him upstairs to her bedroom.

Hours later Patrick left the house in a far

more relaxed state than he had been when he arrived. He carefully backed the Morris off the steps and headed down the road as dusk bathed the fields in a beautiful last light. At the cross-road he paused. Turn left and see Dave and fulfil his promise to Gertrude to warn him, or turn right and head to the local for a counter tea and an evening on the pokies.

He grimaced as he struggled with this choice but no matter how much he had enjoyed Gertrude he still couldn't stomach the idea of Dave as a son in law and so he turned right to an enriching evening of local entertainment, leaving Dave to his fate.

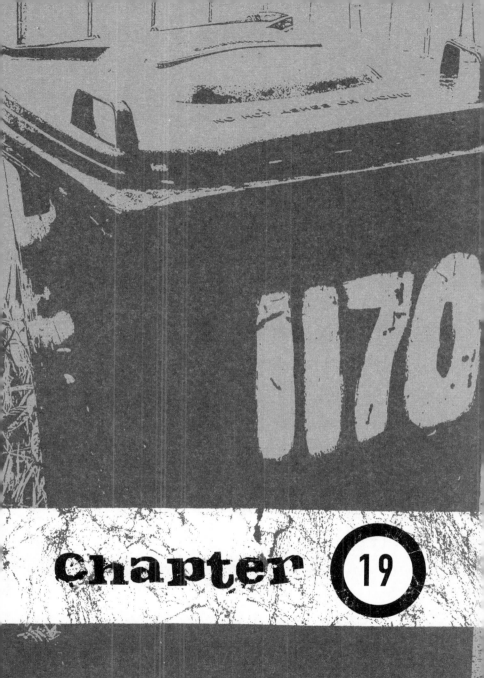

chapter 19

Both Yousef and Achmed's frustration had now reached boiling point. 'We have tried everything to obtain the plutonium from those fools without drawing attention to ourselves but now it is time for attack!' shrieked Yousef, pulling a gun and shooting the motel room's television. This was the fourth television that they had destroyed that week and the manager was starting to question their story of being international Arabic rock and roll stars in hiding.

Achmed looked up from the knife he was so

lovingly sharpening 'The fat one, Dave, he is mine,' he stated, remembering the kick Dave had delivered to his arse and the damage he had taken on their last attempt to get the plutonium. He studied the point of the blade, 'Yes, he is mine and he will die slowly.'

Yousef grinned. 'Alright my friend he is yours but tonight is the last time we will go and get the plutonium no matter what. Agreed?'

'Agreed,' answered Achmed, 'this will be the last time I will have to see that infidel. So let us gather our equipment and prepare for this final assault.'

They spent the next few hours unloading their weapons from a wide variety of hiding spots. The semtex came from the toothpaste tube, the 9mm from the bottom of the suitcase and the knives from under the handle. A camera tripod was cleverly rearranged to form a rifle. Bullets to suit these had been purchased from a local sporting store using a false identity. The man at the store had wondered why two middle-eastern gentlemen required so much ammunition. There were no large kangaroo culls planned that he knew about and it would have to be a pure cull because with those shells there wouldn't be much left to skin. But a sale was a sale and besides the ammo was past its 'use by' date so they would possibly not be back for more.

Yousef and Achmed spent a couple of hours finalising their equipment and preparing a plan of attack. They dressed in their combat suits and red headband and then carefully fitted a range of equipment. First, utility belts and then a shoulder holster; Achmed added a bandolier. By 4 p.m. they were ready and started loading everything else they had prepared into the remaining scooter's sidecar.

Yousef jumped onto the scooter and said 'Let's go, my friend, and take the next step towards our fame.'

Achmed paused, 'Yousef, I think we need to have some more camouflage.' He was right, the sidecar had so many barrels protruding from it that it now resembled an echidna and the sight of a fully armed terrorist riding a scooter was likely to draw a response from some members of the public. So they returned to the motel room to see what else they could use. Many items were considered but in the end they settled for the bathroom robes that were supplied in the room.

A strange sight it was that greeted people who saw them. Two men looking like they'd just stepped from the shower, apart from the black open faced helmets with dark visors, riding on a scooter combination out towards the dump.

Yousef parked approximately 300 metres from the main gate, out of sight, and unloaded whatever they thought would be needed. They waited patiently until it was nearly dusk and the customers had left. They watched as Uri came down and locked the main gate. It would be better to attack now rather than when the customers were here. Not that they cared about anyone, for to them the lives of infidels were meaningless, but it would make the target easier to reach.

* * *

Uri continued to patrol the entrance to the dump. He paced backwards and forwards as he surveyed the scene. All seemed quiet and no sign of the two targets that had been attempting to raid the area. He paused and stood quietly gazing over all the features when his world turned black and he fell face down into the mud.

'Well done, Yousef,' said Achmed. 'I have not seen such a fine shot for many a year.'

Yousef smiled, 'I practiced with stones and my sling for many years on the West Bank against the Israeli soldiers. But that indeed was a fine shot.'

They moved forward to the gate bringing with them a one metre long pair of bolt cutters. These quickly sheared the padlock that held the gates shut. Achmed dropped the bolt cutters and the pair moved silently past the unconscious body of Uri to the shed. They flattened themselves against the wall and listened for any sound.

From deep inside the shack they could hear two voices they assumed were those of the ones called Dave and Slim. They were arguing, as they often did. Yousef and Achmed considered going for a frontal attack on both when they suddenly heard footsteps as one moved to the rear of the shack. A moment later Slim emerged from the rear door and headed to the portaloo at the back of the shack.

Yousef raised the rifle to his shoulder but Achmed stopped him. He put a finger to his lips indicating that he wanted silence. Yousef nodded in agreement and lowered the rifle. Achmed then moved towards Slim's location.

Slim was more concerned about answering a bodily function than he was about anything else and he continued on his trip with a dogged determination oblivious to anything else around him.

Achmed moved into a position behind Slim and was reaching for his knife as Slim entered the portaloo and slammed the door shut. Never one to miss an opportunity Achmed quickly changed his plan and simply slid the padlock bolt across the door, locking Slim inside.

At that moment Dave emerged from the shack ready to give Slim another blast, no matter what his location or position. But instead of seeing Slim he came face to face with Achmed.

Dave screamed at the terrorist at the top of his lungs, 'Who the hell are you and what are you doing in my dump?' He turned, grabbed the tom cat hat and slammed it on his head in an act of defiance, whilst yelling, 'You're not getting my rubbish, you mongrel tip rats!' The sound of a bullet slamming into the doorway next to Dave sent him diving to the ground. 'What the f… !' Dave began to yell, caught in mid-expletive as another bullet splintered more wood from the nearby doorframe.

Obviously these weren't your average tip rats. No way. Most were happy to just grab a car door or bike frame, maybe a motor but obviously these guys wanted a lot more. But what? The mechanical worm? It had to be! Well the bastards weren't going to get it that easily!

Keeping low Dave crawled to the back door and opened it as quietly as he could whilst the sound of more bullets striking the area he had just left echoed through the room. Dave realised that this room wouldn't stop any bullets, the only thing in here solid enough to do that was him, something he wasn't in favour of. He quickly figured that he had to get into the machinery shed where the steel would offer some protection.

Dave stayed low and crawled out the back

door. Damn, he had little to defend himself with. Since the tip had been cleared up he no longer needed the full collection of firearms that had been required to control the variety of pests. Pity, the AK47 he used to use for large rat infestations would have been most welcome about now.

He lifted the lid on the gun box and looked inside. A shotgun, wow, double barrel, yeah, not automatic, damn. 'Oh well it's all I've got,' Dave accepted, and he grabbed it from the box and rammed a couple of shells into it.

Feeling a bit better now that he was armed, Dave cautiously crept along the wall of the hut until he reached the corner closest to the shed. Carefully he peered around and immediately drew a volley of fire. Realising that his cover wouldn't last much longer Dave paused until the firing ceased and then flung himself into action. Breaking from his cover he yelled, 'You won't get me, you bastards!' loosed off the two shotgun shells in the general direction of the terrorists and continued running for the shed. Yousef and Achmed ducked as the pellets whistled over their heads, and once sure that no more were coming, popped up and started shooting at the fleeing figure.

Dave ran for all that he was worth. He knew that it was a gamble but otherwise they were going to take his worm. He was within twenty metres of the shed when they started returning the fire. Dave could feel the bullets creeping up behind him, a line of death that was slowly getting closer as he neared the shed. With five metres to go he knew he wouldn't make it and so tried to dive for cover with the aim of completing a graceful somersault into the shed.

Instead, it was more like a disastrous three-and-a-half-turn flop, occasionally in the pike position with the limbs following in no specific fashion. It was sort of like watching a dog that has just been hit by a speeding car tumble to the kerb side. But it worked.

At least here he had some hope. If he could board the composter he could use that to provide him some cover whilst he escaped. Although it would not exactly be an inconspicuous escape it would be an escape. Wasting no time he climbed up the stairs and entered the cabin.

'Come on you bastard!' Dave screamed as the starter whirred. After what seemed a lifetime the motor finally caught and Dave's hopes soared with the engine revs. He reached down and engaged the drive at the same time he heard the sound of the first bullet ricocheting off the steel structure. But he was committed now and there was nowhere to go but out into the field of fire and so he ducked down as low as possible, clenched his teeth and moved the composter out into the open.

The sound in the cabin was enormous as a hail of bullets hit from the right hand side, the windows shattered and glass flew everywhere. He could feel the machine lurch as a bullet punctured the right hand tractor tyre. But stopping was not an option and so he ploughed on.

Dave couched down low into the composter's cabin and valiantly tried to steer it back onto course, but as the tyre slowly deflated it became more and more difficult. He heaved on the steering wheel but the machine was getting slow to respond. It was becoming clear that in a very short time it would be uncontrollable and that now his only hope of survival would be to get to his ute. But how could he get there? He needed a diversion, so he reached across and engaged the mulching part of the composter, which started to spew out compost and dust as it gobbled up anything that was in its way.

'Now,' he said quietly, 'that will provide some cover for a short time but I've got to find a way out.'

There was a small furrow in the ground some metres to his right, an area that he remembered from his school cadet days as being 'in defilade', meaning providing cover from fire and view if you were crawling along it. A little bit further away was his ute. If he could crawl along that furrow he could make it to the ute unseen and make a getaway before these Arab lunatics knew where he was. He decided to go for it, as he was staring certain death in the face if he remained with the composter.

He jumped from the composter's cabin and ran the two metres to the furrow, dropping down like a dog with a severed carotid artery, his chest making contact with what looked like a bucket of tripe but was actually a decomposing kangaroo carcass. He slithered along on the slime of it's maggot infested sheen and then came up hard against a rock, cursing as he cut his wrist on a sharp edge of quartz.

Like a rat up a drainpipe he leopard crawled in style and with the speed that only the fear of a bullet up his brown eye could create. In no time at all he was at the end of the furrow. The firing from Yousef's armaments had ceased as the Arab realised that his quarry had somehow disappeared. It wouldn't take long for the hunters to pick up his trail again though, Dave considered. Time to make the open cover dash to the ute. He prayed that the bloody thing would start first time, very glad that he always left his keys in the ignition.

Meanwhile Yousef had realised how Dave had escaped, well in tune to the advantages of concealed ground, from his days in the training camps in Libya. He instinctively recognised that the ute was where Dave would go next and he ran around in the opposite direction to get there first.

As Dave appeared, only a few feet away he saw the ugly grinning face of his adversary. Dave couldn't believe his getaway plan had been foiled.

He was cornered, his back pressed into the bonnet of the ute and nowhere left to run. Yousef grinned and moved slowly towards him.

'Now infidel you will give me the plutonium,' said Yousef.

'What plutonium?' screamed Dave, 'I don't have any of that sort of shit here.' Yousef raised the gun to his hip so that the muzzle pointed at Dave. 'Well if you will not help then I will kill you slowly,' and Yousef fired a shot that grazed Dave's left hip.

Meanwhile the composter continued to circle around its deflated tyre, slowly moving in small steps towards them. As it came closer it finally came in contact with a large engine block, which stopped the good tyre from rotating. This forced the machine to spin around in the other direction whilst the good tyre kept trying to climb the obstacle in front of it.

Dave clutched his side in pain and Yousef grinned and moved closer. 'That is but a taste of what is come,' he said through clenched teeth. Behind them the composter continued to turn in the opposite direction until it finally cleared the engine block and resumed its right hand circling on a new axis, one that put it on a collision course with Dave and Yousef.

Dave looked at his hand, which was now covered with blood, and then up at Yousef. 'You piece of scum! I wouldn't give you the steam off my shit.'

Yousef just grinned 'Oh no, my friend, you will give me so much more than that.'

Dave looked up and saw the composter swinging around towards them. He quickly calculated the turning radius and was sure that the machine was going to come in their direction. If he could just keep this killer talking here long enough he might just have a chance to survive.

'What is it that you want, you prick?' asked Dave.

'Plutonium,' answered Yousef. 'We know you have it, Henri told us. Now where is it?'

'Henri?' said Dave in some confusion. So, that little French prick was behind all this. He looked up at the composter that was drawing nearer and calculated that another minute should do it.

It was time to bluff like he'd never bluffed before. 'Are you talking about Henri in Paris? Why you stupid bastard, that prick's dudded you. He works for the CIA, didn't you know that?' Dave sweated as he prayed that this would keep the Arab guessing, for just a little longer.

Yousef was thinking fast, his paranoia assisting him to almost believe Dave's bluff. 'What are you talking about, you filthy infidel vermin?'

'Henri works for the bloody CIA. His sister's married to one of their field operatives. He's in the anti-terrorist squad. His mother's an American. His brother was killed by the Vietcong. His brother's mate flew missions into Afghanistan. His girlfriend's a weapons instructor with the US Navy, his best mate's...'

Yousef cut off Dave's increasingly unbelievable diatribe. 'Enough!' he screamed. 'You lie, and you will die,' he said as he lifted his weapon for the final burst that would kill Dave as dead as the decomposing possum's scrotum that was rotting on the sole of his boot.

Dave only needed a few seconds more of distraction. He did what didn't come naturally, he started to laugh and giggle, 'Ha ha ha...' he began, 'don't you realise, ha, ha... that Henri... heh, heh...he set you up, ha, ha, hic,' he finally gulped, his eyes bulging.

Yousef spun around to see what Dave was laughing at and realised that he had nowhere to go. He threw has hands over his face as the composter bore down on him knocking him to the ground. The first of the blades struck home, instantly composting his right foot, and then his thigh and then his other foot. Yousef screamed but the machine kept moving on up his body slowly chewing him away just like people do to a Teddy Bear biscuit that had been dunked in coffee.

Dave in the meantime jumped over the bonnet of his ute and hobbled back to the shack. He paused to watch as the machine continued to eat Yousef until only his head was left. Dave watched, smiling as the last thing to go through Yousef's mind was one of his metal compost blades.

But the composter didn't finish there. Having digested Yousef it continued on its path of destruction and attempted to eat Dave's ute. The scream of tearing metal was incredible as the two machines met and attempted to destroy each other. It ruptured the petrol lines on the ute and the associated sparks created a fire which engulfed both machines. Finally the composter could chew no more and stalled, and the two machines froze in their deadly embrace whilst the fire continued to try and consume what remained of them.

Dave shivered and slumped back against the wall as the intensity of the moment and the pain from his injury washed over him like a tidal wave. But this was no time to relax. There was still one of those bloody tip rats out there trying to kill him and it seemed as if he would stop at nothing. That was very obvious, he considered as he felt his hip; yeah, definitely obvious. But where was the piece of foreign excrement? With the ute smashed there was no way out so it was going to be a fight to the end.

But Dave was in no condition to fight; his leg hurt like hell and he had no weapons. It was obvious that these guys were not just tip rats. They were at the very least well-armed tip rats, perhaps even ex-military. It was also obvious that they wanted him, dead or alive, and from the look of it they seemed to prefer more dead than alive. But at least one of them was down, which helped even the odds but Dave was still up against a formidable enemy. Blind Freddie could tell that.

'Bloody hell,' he whispered, 'where's Slim or Uri? I could really use a hand here.'

Dave let out a huge fart of relief, partly from desire but largely uncontrolled. 'Shit,' he said to himself, which was close to the mark. Unfortunately the discernible ripping sound alerted Achmed to his whereabouts, and the pungent odour that followed the sound allowed Dave's second adversary to track straight to him.

Achmed stuck his head slightly above a mound of putrescent filth and rotting cardboard covered in snails and smiled grimly as he saw Dave partly hidden just a few metres away. He aimed his weapon and prepared to fire a shot that would decorate Dave's head with a third eye. Unfortunately the slimy surface he was propped upon warmed under his shoes and he slid a few centimetres just as his finger pressure increased on the trigger. The shot went high, but still parted what was left of Dave's hair.

'Holy shit!' Dave exclaimed, dropping immediately to the ground and then cursing himself for not picking a place out of the line of fire. He heard an Arab curse and managed to get back onto his feet just as he saw Achmed appear over the top of the mound to his left, with a small rifle in his hands. Dave dived to the ground as a second bullet whizzed past his now prone form. He felt vulnerable, potentially doomed even, but managed to get his legs working again and started to run.

It was too late. Achmed had anticipated his direction and jumped down from the mound and called out to his victim, 'Stop there. There is no point in running away my friend,' Achmed sneered.

Dave knew he was done for, but the preservation instinct is strong and he still hoped for a way out. Achmed walked slowly towards him as Dave fell over, hard, and rolled over onto his back and started to crawl backwards away from Achmed and his frightening manic eyes, until his back hit the tank he had used for the worms, trapping him with nowhere to go. Achmed looked down the barrel of the gun, the sights squarely centred in between the glazed cat's eyes on Dave's forehead.

'Now infidel, forget the plutonium, this is personal for what you did to both Yousef and me and so now, you die,' he said.

Dave's eyes turned away; he knew that this was it. He looked to the ground and saw a disturbance in the soil as something was about to break through. Achmed started to pull the trigger but he was jerked to the side by the movement of a giant earthworm, now the size of an anaconda, which erupted from the ground at his feet. The worm wrapped itself around him pinning the gun to his side.

Dave looked on in amazement. There was something familiar about this worm, but he had never seen anything like it. But it still seemed that he should know it.

'Red?' asked Dave. 'Is that you? But you're only supposed to be this long,' said Dave holding up his thumb and index finger.

The worm raised part of itself, whilst still keeping Achmed pinned to the ground, and moved its head closer to Dave's. They stared at each other for a while until Red released a belch and a vile yellow liquid coated Dave.

'It is you!' yelled Dave and launched himself at Red, throwing his arms around the worm and hugging it intensely. Red entwined himself around Dave as well while Achmed, now also covered in the yellow slime, vomited up what-ever was left in his stomach.

This was the strange scene that greeted Uri as he regained consciousness. Indeed it took another five minutes before he could actually believe that what he saw was real rather than an extension of the hallucinations that he had been seeing whilst unconscious.

He staggered to his feet and in halting, bum-bling steps moved towards the strange group. Not one to loose an opportunity, no matter how bizarre, he removed the gun from Achmed's hand and then using a pair of handcuffs that he had concealed on his belt he secured him so that he could cause no more trouble. The worm sensed that Achmed was no longer a problem and so instead dedicated its entire interest to playing with Dave.

Uri was stunned. So this was the secret of the dump, this must have been what the terrorists were after all the time. Imagine what such a creature could do. It would be capable of under-mining any defences, it could provide a stealth attack on any target and then there were the ecological benefits. With the volume of vermi-cast that could be produced it would be possible to rebuild countless areas of what is currently desert. But in the wrong hands the worm could undermine complete cities and collapse them and it was always out of sight. Awesome!

What a weapon, no wonder they had been so determined to get it at any cost. With this the World Trade Centre attack could be made to look like nothing. A weapon like this could undermine a whole city and they would never know until it was far too late. Yes, Godzilla would seem like a friendly tourist compared to what this worm could do. Uri realised then that he had to obtain this worm for his country no matter what.

'Dave,' said Uri, 'what is this thing, is it your pet?'

'Ummff, nggg rdd,' answered Dave, now buried under the undivided attention of a very friendly worm.

Uri tried again, 'Dave, do you know this worm?'

Dave managed to turn his head so that he could speak. 'Yeah, he's mine, the name's Red, I gu...' The conversation paused there as Red continued to show its extreme affection for Dave by trying to place his head in Dave's mouth.

But Uri was not going to be diverted from the discussion. 'Dave,' he said 'I must have this worm, it is ideal for my country, it could have so many benefits.'

Dave, who was now half buried under the worm, was having trouble seeing the benefits of owning such a worm and was a little taken aback by this statement. Still, not one to pass an opportunity by, he wriggled his head clear and looked at Uri and said 'What's it worth to you?'

Uri paused, how do you put a value on the ultimate weapon, the ultimate land reclaimer and recycler? It's worth was incalculable! So where do you start the negotiation? Trillions? Billions? Millions?

'Dave,' started Uri, 'I will make you one offer only, so listen carefully. I will give you five million US dollars for the worm, plus I will take care of the mess that is here including this scum,' he said pointing to Achmed. 'But you must tell no one of this nor must you ever breed another worm like him, do you understand?'

Dave just nodded, actually he hadn't heard a thing after the bit about five million US dollars. He was in shock, not surprisingly given all that had just happened, but never one to let an opportunity pass by he muttered, 'OK you've got a deal,' and extracted himself out from underneath the worm.

Uri was ecstatic. He had procured the ultimate weapon for a bargain basement price. Now all he had to do was to work out how to move the worm to Israel and to clean up the mess left by the terrorists so that all involved were happy and no-one outside would suspect anything. With a sense of relief sweeping over him, Dave felt his bladder finally starting to give after such a traumatic event and so headed to the lavatory. The old portaloo had suffered a bit from the battle. It was leaning to one side and a number of bullet holes now dotted the once pristine structure. He unbolted the padlock bolt and opened the door. There was Slim, frozen in position, pants around his ankles surrounded by a number of bullet holes. Dave stared at him, 'Hurry up ya bastard, will ya!' he said and slammed the door. This had the effect of galvanising Slim into action. It seemed that the fight must have been over and that meant that he no longer had to sit here feeling like one of those magician's assistants who have swords stuck through a box they're in. Swords might have been better because it was not pleasant sitting there and suddenly watching holes appear around you never knowing if the next one would be through you.

Slim put down his now perforated copy of Penthouse, pausing for a moment to admire the accuracy of the bullet that had punctured Miss September, then cleaned himself up and exited the portaloo.

'About frigging time!' yelled Dave as he pushed Slim aside and rushed in.

Slim surveyed the dump taking in the burning composter and ute, the giant worm, and that strange Arab man from a couple of days ago in handcuffs with Uri standing over him. Slim scratched his head and said, 'Did I miss something?'

Chapter 20

THE LOCAL PAPER CAME OUT THE FOLLOWING day and it ran the banner heading 'Rock Star Tragedy - One killed, other seriously injured'. It was a calamity that the whole area felt. Two such great stars of the stage cut down in their prime whilst holidaying in their area. The mayor featured prominently in the paper, proposing a statue to the pair and a memorial rock concert to be held at a disused soccer ground. On the second page of the paper was another major story, this time dealing with a significant export contract that had been let to a local transport company to fly a large quantity of goods from the town to Israel.

Meanwhile over the next few weeks everything started to return to 'normal' life. The dump had been swamped with local tourists who wanted to know about the rock stars and what sort of accident they had had at the dump. After telling the story so many times, Dave had perfected the tale of how they had come here seeking solitude and a place to film their new video but unfortunately due to the combination of sex, drugs and rock and roll they had been inspired to invade the dump. Here they had met their untimely demise by playing with machinery for which they had not been trained. An unfortunate accident in which it was assumed that they had tried to play 'chicken' using the composter and Dave's ute. Dave had also set up a souvenir stall at the dump with snowballs that when shaken had two Arabic looking men in the dump being surrounded by swirls of scrap paper. The CD by the 'Terrorists', actually a local band who took advantage of the situation, was also selling well and Dave was happy to autograph a copy for every customer. But with the composter destroyed the dump had again started to return to its old self and this was slowing down business. The odours, birds and vermin had also returned. Yes it was a return to the 'good old days' but Dave had even more important things on his mind.

* * *

Keith, the motel owner was also happy. When he had first heard the news he was deeply upset as it seemed unlikely that he would get paid for the outstanding bill. But the nice men he assumed were from the funeral parlour, as they were dressed in black, wore sunglasses and had a slight accent, came and paid all that was owed and a touch more.

* * *

Slim who was now also returning to normal, apart from a strong dislike for using portapotties, settled back and read the paper whilst drinking a glass to their 'friends' memory at the newly installed 'Ben Gurion' bar at the football club. Slim sighed, who'd have imagined that Uri was both rich and an Australian rules football fan. He raised his glass again, amazed at the benefits multiculturalism had brought to his club. 'Gonna miss him,' he said aloud to no one in particular and drained the glass.

* * *

Uri was also happy now he was back in Israel. He'd returned to a hero's welcome amongst the intelligence community. But it was the simple pleasures of fresh air and no rubbish that most appealed to him. But he had one piece of unfinished business still to take care off. He picked up the phone and dialled a number and a sleepy female voice answered, 'Yes'.

'Nefertiti, this is Uri, the target is eliminated. Please move on to the next item.' With that he hung up.

* * *

Achmed on the other hand was not happy. He was receiving the best hospital care available and his body was slowly recovering from the onslaught. His hosts were greatly concerned about his well being as they wanted him to be in perfect health before they trialed and executed him. 'That infidel Dave is behind all of this and I swear by all that is evil that I shall avenge myself on him!' he screamed, as he had done continuously since his arrival.

* * *

It was over. Dave slumped in his chair, which by now had a distinct lean to one side due to the consumption of most of the right hand side frame by termites. My God, what an experience, he thought. In the last couple of weeks he'd been shot at, attacked, dragged before numerous agencies and spewed on by a worm. Actually Dave felt a little bit of loss now that Red was gone but when confronted with lots of guys dressed in black with sunglasses and a bulge under their armpits, well you tend not to argue. He glanced around the shack and paused at the numerous bullet holes that had been recently added to the decor and shivered. He had come so close, so many times. The bastards had even invaded his home. They'd killed Cutie, which hadn't bothered him, but dumping the body in his bed was a bit rude. He still woke with nightmares about waking up in bed with that mongrel dog also in there, poised and ready to strike.

At least Uri had assured him that Henri had now been returned to complete his outstanding five years in the French Foreign Legion. Somehow the thought of that froggie bastard spending time in the desert sun, preferably staked out on top of a sand dune, really appealed now, because whichever way you looked at it he had started this whole thing off.

But now what? He'd gone full circle and now was back at the stage of having a dump that was nearly full and his composter was shattered beyond recognition. The hulk still sat outside the window where it had landed, smoking gracefully from a number of parts. Still the money from Uri was good, perhaps now he could build another house behind the first. Maybe make it four stories high so that Mum couldn't see the hills from his first house. It was a good idea and Dave smiled to himself but then again facing Mum would be more frightening than those terrorists. Still, encouraged by his survival of this episode maybe he should press his luck. Yeah a nice new house with a couple of pig pens out the front.

But as far as the dump was concerned it was time for a new plan, perhaps something a little less ambitious this time. But what could he do to bring in an income without filling up the dump? It would need something where all the parts could be converted into product and flogged to the punters, hopefully at a good margin. He relaxed back in the chair and scratched his balls. At half stroke he paused and then leaped into the air shouting, 'Why not?' and scrambled for his phone.

A minute later he was talking to his politician contact, the one who'd financed his last trip to Paris. It took some haggling and some threats but in the end he won the agreement he wanted. Slamming the phone down with glee he then dialled a second number and waited impatiently, tapping his fingers on the table until the call was answered.

'Yes?' a sweet voice said.

'Caroline, it's Dave. Guess what?' he asked.

'Just tell me, Dave, you know I don't like to play games, well, not on the phone anyway. Are you coming over?' she asked.

'Better than that. We're going to take a little trip together, all expenses paid. We're going overseas, to look at pig farms with methane electricity generators attached to them,' he said.

Caroline didn't answer for a few seconds, so Dave continued.

'It's a study tour, Caroline.'

'Why would we want to do that, Dave?' she asked.

'Why? Why? Well, why not?' he asked with some irritation.

'I'm not the studying type of girl, Dave, you know that,' she argued.

Dave laughed, 'No, no, you silly little thing. Not that kind of study tour. We'll be looking at piggeries, together, staying in hotel rooms, together, learning all sorts of things, together…' he paused.

'Dave,' she began, 'Is there another word for this kind of trip?'

'What do you mean?' he asked, completely dumbfounded.

'Oh, I don't know…honey,' she said.

'Umm,' he hesitated.

'Did you see the moon tonight, honey?' she cooed.

'The moon?'

'Yes, the moon…honey,' she persisted.

She's never called me honey before, and what's with the bloody moon. 'Oh shit,' he gulped.

'Are you alright, Dave? The trip sounds lovely. Of course I can't see dad agreeing, what with a single girl going away with a man, alone, un-chaperoned and all,' she suggested. 'Oh honey, the moon is so large tonight.'

Dave was slow, but even his brain cells eventually made the connection. Well, why not, he thought. He loved her. There, he'd said it now. It was true, she was the only girl for him, always had been.

'Caroline?' he began.

'Yes, honey?' she purred.

He gulped, took a deep breath and plunged in. 'Will you marry me?' he asked.

'Oh, Dave,' she squealed. 'Oh course I will.' Then after a small pause she said, 'Dave, that means that we could make this study tour our honeymoon.'

'What about your father?' Dave asked.

'Don't worry about him, Dave. I'll make the wedding arrangements and he'll be okay about it all. Anyway, he seems to have mellowed a little lately. Seems he's meeting some woman at night, three times a week. Of course I'm not supposed to know about it. Not sure who she is but who cares as long as he stays out of our way, eh? Oh, Dave, married life will be wonderful for us,' she cooed once more.

'Caroline?'

'Yes, my darling?'

'Is he there now?'

'No he's out. Why? Are you coming over?' she asked.

'Definitely!' he shouted, his left hand rubbing his crotch.

'Dave, my fiancé is always welcome here. Are you coming now?'

'God, how did you know?' he asked, embarrassed.

She giggled. 'Drive carefully,' she said and then heard the phone line drop out.

As Dave was driving out to the farm he laughed, somewhat hysterically. 'Married, ha! I'm getting married. Now where will we go on our honeymoon? Not bloody France,' he said, his grin widening. 'Anywhere but France.'

EPILOGUE

EPILOGUE

A FEW WEEKS BEFORE THE WEDDING, DAVE SAT back in the dump listening to the TV, which was broadcasting stories about increases in land subsidence in Palestine that was being attributed to sudden increases in agricultural output in Israel. Dave shrugged, somehow these things seemed all so distant and irrelevant to him and his dump. His main concern was that the dump was now just about at the point of overflowing. Mind you, after what he'd been through, nothing seemed critical any more. All of his problems were gone, except that the dump was full. Even the EPA was at last off his back, as were customs, the terrorists, and all of those government types in black suits asking daft questions. It also seemed as if Henri had been contacted by some old French Foreign Legion buddies, according to Uri.

No, nothing was critical any more.

But Dave was wrong. For deep in the dump those little steel boxes had succumbed to the onslaught of the material that they had contained for so long and now the contents were merging into a mass that was indeed 'critical.'

And life at the dump, like Dave's own life, would possibly never be the same again. But that's another story.

New Releases…Also from Sid Harta Publishers

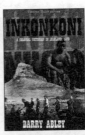

SEE OVERLEAF FOR MORE NEW RELEASES!

OTHER BEST SELLING SID HARTA TITLES CAN BE FOUND AT

http://www.sidharta.com.au   http://Anzac.sidharta.com

***

HAVE YOU WRITTEN A STORY!

http://www.publisher-guidelines.com
for manuscript guideline submissions

***

LOOKING FOR A PUBLISHER!

http://www.temple-house.com

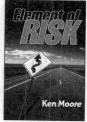

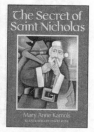

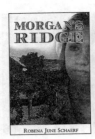

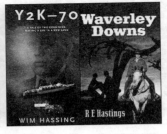

Best-selling titles by Kerry B. Collison

Readers are invited to visit our publishing websites at:
http://www.sidharta.com.au
http://www.publisher-guidelines.com/
http://temple-house.com/

Kerry B. Collison's home pages:
http://www.authorsden.com/visit/uthor.asp?AuthorID=2239
http://www.expat.or.id/sponsors/collison.html
http://clubs.yahoo.com/clubs/asianintelligencesresources
email: author@sidharta.com.au